Beginning OpenOffice Calc

From Setting Up Simple Spreadsheets
to Business Forecasting

Jacek Artymiak

Apress®

Beginning OpenOffice Calc: From Setting Up Simple Spreadsheets to Business Forecasting

ISBN-13 (pbk): 978-1-4302-3159-2

ISBN-13 (electronic): 978-1-4302-3160-8

President and Publisher: Paul Manning
Lead Editor: Matt Wade
Technical Reviewers: Bruce Byfield and Steve Potts
Editorial Board: Steve Anglin, Mark Beckner, Ewan Buckingham, Gary Cornell, Jonathan Gennick, Jonathan Hassell, Michelle Lowman, James Markham, Matthew Moodie, Jeff Olson, Jeffrey Pepper, Frank Pohlmann, Douglas Pundick, Ben Renow-Clarke, Dominic Shakeshaft, Matt Wade, Tom Welsh
Coordinating Editor: Annie Beck
Copy Editor: Barbara Stiegelbauer
Production Support: Patrick Cunningham
Indexer: BiM Indexing & Proofreading Services
Artist: SPI Global
Cover Designer: Anna Ishchenko

Distributed to the book trade worldwide by Springer Science+Business Media, LLC., 233 Spring Street, 6th Floor, New York, NY 10013. Phone 1-800-SPRINGER, fax (201) 348-4505, e-mail orders-ny@springer-sbm.com, or visit www.springeronline.com.

For information on translations, please e-mail rights@apress.com, or visit www.apress.com.

Apress and friends of ED books may be purchased in bulk for academic, corporate, or promotional use. eBook versions and licenses are also available for most titles. For more information, reference our Special Bulk Sales–eBook Licensing web page at www.apress.com/bulk-sales.

Contents at a Glance

Contents

About the Author

Jacek Artymiak has written more than 100 articles and more than a dozen books on Linux, OpenBSD, OpenOffice.org, Open Source, firewalls, networking, security, and system administration.

Preface

Functions and formulas are the secret weapon in every spreadsheet user's arsenal. They help you quickly analyze huge amounts of data or build interactive models that let you try different scenarios before you commit your time and money to a project.

If you ever want to compare prices or financing options, or find out when you are going to break even, you should be using formulas to make such analysis as easy as punching different numbers into the spreadsheet.

I wrote this book to help you learn quickly how to use functions and formulas in OpenOffice.org Calc. It is not a long book because I want you to get up to speed as fast as possible.

I hope you will find this book a valuable resource.

CHAPTER 1

Essentials

In this chapter you will learn the basics of working with data in OpenOffice.org Calc—how to enter, edit, organize, and format information.

To get the best out of the information presented in this book, especially when you are just beginning to learn OpenOffice.org Calc, you might want to create a new worksheet to experiment with the tools and the techniques described on the following pages.

Creating a New Worksheet

You can create a new worksheet in a number of ways, but selecting **File ➤ New ➤ Spreadsheet** is probably the most convenient way of doing it from any OpenOffice.org module (see Figure 1-1).

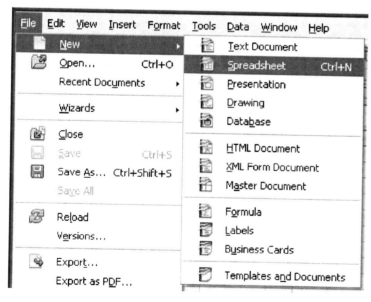

Figure 1-1. *Creating a new worksheet*

Pressing **Ctrl+N** is also a handy shortcut when you already are working in Calc.

Entering Data

Entering information into an OpenOffice.org Calc worksheet is generally a matter of double-clicking on a cell and typing whatever it is you wish to type. A single hit on the **Enter/Return** key stores your input inside the current cell.

Pressing one of the cursor (arrows) keys on the keyboard or clicking on another cell has the same effect unless you are entering a formula, in which case OpenOffice.org Calc will insert references to the cells to which you moved the spreadsheet cursor. To get out of that mode, press **Esc**.

The spreadsheet cursor is the thick, black frame around a cell. The text cursor is the black, vertical bar that moves across the screen as you type.

OpenOffice.org Calc is smart enough to recognize many popular types of data (numbers, money, dates, text, etc.). Whatever you type into a cell appears inside that cell and on the **Input Line** field located at the top of the worksheet area.

The **Input Line** is a useful feedback tool. If something doesn't look right inside a cell, the **Input Line** will always show you its raw, unformatted content.

The **Input Line** is also a convenient place to edit data.

To edit data stored inside a cell, do any of the following actions: double-click on it, press **F2**, or click once on the **Input Line**.

Figure 1-2. *The **Input Line** (the field in the top right corner) is both a feedback window and a cell editing field.*

How OpenOffice.org Calc Treats Your Input

OpenOffice.org Calc uses an elaborate set of rules to determine how to classify and display the information you store inside a worksheet. Most of those rules are fairly straightforward, and as long as you properly set the operating system's local settings for date and money formatting, whatever you type or paste ought to be interpreted in the right way.

The following sections explain how OpenOffice.org Calc treats each type of data. Read them if you want to understand why your input is being interpreted, displayed, and printed the way it is. You will also pick up tips on forcing OpenOffice.org Calc to interpret your input in the way you think is correct.

Text

Entering text into a cell is as straightforward as it can possibly be. Just double-click on a cell, type whatever you want to type, and then hit the **Enter/Return** key.

OpenOffice.org Calc is smart enough to tell the difference between dates, formulas, numbers, text, and time. When it gets confused and does not understand your input one way or another, it will treat what you type as text. For example, **Annual Report**, **Year 2010 Sales in Omaha**, **1st Quarter Results**, and **2010 Sales Summary** are all treated as text.

You can force OpenOffice.org Calc to treat any kind of input as a string of text by placing a single quote (') in front of it. Type **1000** and **'1000** into two separate cells to see the difference for yourself (see Figure 1-3).

Figure 1-3. Forcing numbers to be treated as text

Spelling Correction

Every time you type some text, it is possible that you will make spelling mistakes. OpenOffice.org Calc can correct them automatically, or you can turn auto correction off and only run the checks when you are ready to do so.

The default setting is to spell-check everything you type. If OpenOffice.org Calc finds either something you misspelled or something it thinks you misspelled, then it will underline that part of the text using a red line.

	A	B
1	xYz	Parot
2		
3		

Figure 1-4. OpenOffice.org Calc underlines incorrectly spelled words.

To correct the mistake, click on the cell where the underlined text resides and edit it (see section "Editing Data").

What if what you typed is correct and OpenOffice.org Calc does not understand it, because it simply does not have it in its dictionary? You have two choices. If the offending word is a funky name like "xYz," then you can either tell OpenOffice.org Calc to ignore it altogether or add it to the application's dictionary so it knows how to spell it correctly. In either case, what you need to do is double-click on the cell where the underlined text is stored, right-click on the underlined word, and choose either the Add or Ignore All option.

*Figure 1-5. Choose **Add** or **Ignore All** to either add or ignore words.*

OpenOffice.org Calc gives you an option to add words to three dictionaries. Choose soffice.dic.

When you work with large documents or on one of those slightly underpowered netbooks that have become so popular of late, you may want to turn spell-check off. Choose Tools ➤ Options ➤ Language Settings ➤ Writing Aids and uncheck all items in the Options list.

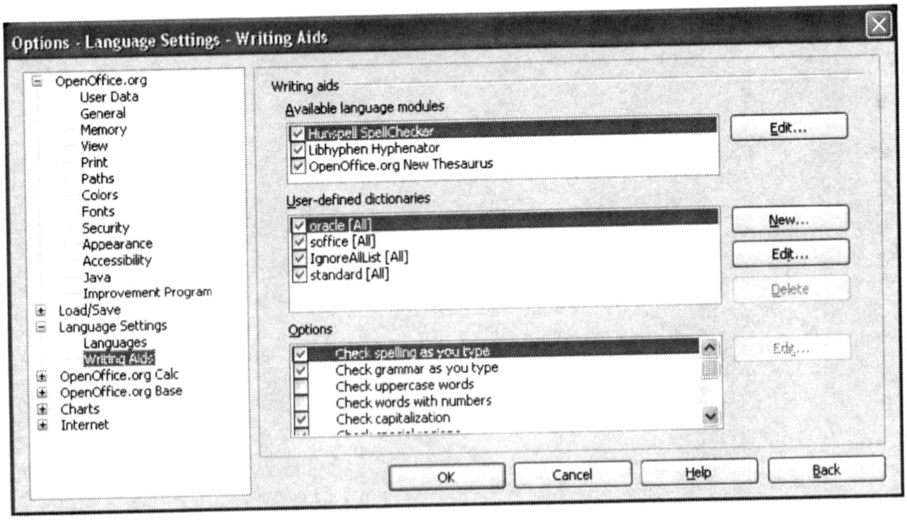

![Options - Language Settings - Writing Aids dialog box]

Figure 1-6. Text correction options

Once you turn off text correction tools, OpenOffice.org Calc should work a tiny bit faster, but it is now up to you to remember to spell-check the document. You do this by pressing F7.

Numbers

Numbers are a bit more complex to handle. If you ever get confused by the way OpenOffice.org Calc interprets your input, here is a list of rules that will help you understand what is happening:

- If you enter anything that resembles a number, it will be interpreted as you would expect. So **1000**, **1.23**, and **1.44444** are all stored and displayed as ordinary integer or floating-point (fractional) numbers.

- Any number that is preceded by the dollar sign (**$**) is treated as a currency value and will be formatted using the currency style. So **$1000000** will be displayed as **$1,000,000.00**. (Styles and formatting are discussed in Chapter 4.)

- You can separate thousands with the comma sign (**,**), as in **1,000,000**, but not with a period (**.**), which is reserved for the decimal point. Numbers with commas but without the dollar sign in front of them are displayed as ordinary numbers—the commas will be removed and the decimal point will stay in its place. This behavior varies depending on the regional settings, as some counties use periods (.) to separate thousands and commas (,) to indicate the decimal point.

- A number followed by the percent sign (**%**) is treated as a percentage value. For example, **10.25%** is shown exactly as you type it in, which is useful if you do not have the time to convert percentages to their fractional equivalents.

- It is OK to use common fractions. You see these numbers fairly often if you work with or invest in securities. Remember to put a space between the integer part and the fraction, as in **12 3/4**. Use the slash sign (**/**) to separate the numerator from the denominator.

- Whenever you enter a common fraction, OpenOffice.org Calc turns it into a decimal fraction to speed up internal calculations. Don't worry. The cell that stores the original input will still display it as a common fraction. The **Input Line** shows the fraction after conversion.

- You can change the number of decimal places shown in cells. You will find the necessary information in Chapter 4.

- Scientific exponential notation, such as **10e12** or **–27.4567e–45**, is permitted.

- Placing the minus sign (–) in front of a number turns it into a negative number.

For more information about the precision of calculations, see the "Numeric Formats" section in Chapter 4.

For more tips on formatting numbers, see the "Numeric Formats" section in Chapter 4.

Dates

Series of numbers separated with a slash (**/**), a period (.), or a hyphen (-) are treated as calendar dates, if they fall within certain limits (see Chapter 12).

For example, **12/29/2010**, **12.29.2010**, and **12-29-2010** are all interpreted by OpenOffice.org Calc as December 29, 2000, but **12-000/23/19345** will be interpreted as text.

To force OpenOffice.org Calc to interpret the numbers that look like calendar dates as text, put a single quote (') in front of the number; for example, type **'12/29/2010** instead of **12/29/2010**.

Date formatting for display depends on the operating system's local settings. Internally, the dates you enter are stored in the same format.

It is a good idea to get used to typing the year in dates as a four-digit number and not as the commonly used two-digit number. This prevents subtle errors caused by the computer misinterpreting dates.

Time

Any series of numbers separated with one or two colons (:) will be interpreted as a time value. For example, **12:13** is displayed as **12:13:00**. Similarly, **9:4:34** is displayed as **9:04:34**. You can even enter **9582:3566:23445345** and OpenOffice.org Calc will convert it into the proper number of hours, minutes, and seconds, but **2:432:7:33** (notice the third colon) is assumed to represent a string of text. Minutes and seconds are always displayed as two-digit numbers.

If you want to prevent OpenOffice.org Calc from automatically interpreting what you entered as a time value, place a single quote (') in front of the time string, as in **'97:45:18**.

Editing Data

We all make mistakes. Not necessarily because we are careless, but because working with numbers is a rather tedious affair and there are plenty of opportunities to introduce errors. Fortunately, they can be easily corrected at any time.

Correcting or changing the content of a worksheet is called *editing*. You can tell that you are in the editing mode when you see the black rectangular cursor change into a text cursor inside the current cell. Another indicator of working in the editing mode is the content "spill" to the neighboring cells (see Figure 1-7). However, don't count on it happening at all times, as you can turn it off by turning on the cell content wrap mode.

Figure 1-7. Editing text stored inside a cell

Here are a few tips on editing data in OpenOffice.org Calc:

- To enter the edit mode, select a cell using the mouse or the keyboard cursor keys and then either double-click on it or press **F2**.

- You can move about inside a cell using the **Left** and **Right** keyboard cursor keys.

- The **Up** and **Down** cursor keys should not be used, as they move the spreadsheet cursor (the thick, black rectangular frame) to the preceding cell or following current one.

- Press **Shift+7** or **Shift+3** to select a portion of the cell's content. Press **Ctrl+A** to select all of it.

- Use **Ctrl+C**, **Ctrl+X**, and **Ctrl+V** to copy, cut, and paste the selected content.

- Use the **Ctrl+Enter** keyboard shortcut to insert line breaks.

- The **Enter/Return** key is used to end the cell edit mode and store the changes you have made inside the current cell.

- If you want to abandon all of your changes while you are still in the edit mode, press **Esc**.

- Undoing recent changes after you hit the **Enter/Return** key is done in the usual way by using the **Ctrl+Z** keyboard shortcut.

- When you are editing long pieces of text or complex formulas, you might want to do your edits on the **Input Line** (located above the active sheet). It will be more comfortable than editing inside the cell itself.

Search and Replace

If you want to do wholesale changes to your spreadsheet, use the **Search** and **Replace** functionality of OpenOffice.org Calc. In order to do that, press Ctrl+F to display the **Find & Replace** dialog. It is a two-mode dialog; you can use it to just search for strings of text or do search and replace. You control its behavior with the **Find, Find Next, Replace,** and **Replace All buttons.**

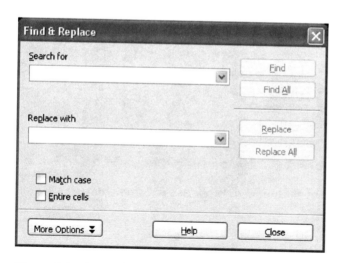

Figure 1-8. The **Find & Replace** dialog

The **Replace** with field does not have to be empty if you want to use **Find Next** to skip a few matching strings. The contents will get used only when you click on the **Replace** or **Replace All** buttons.

Do not worry if you accidentally replace something you did not mean to replace. Simply press **Esc** and then **Ctrl+Z** to revert the changes.

Adding Comments to Cells

A well-designed worksheet ought to be self-explanatory and you should not need to add a lot of extra comments to it, but there are plenty of situations when you want to add additional information not meant to be visible when you print or show your data to others.

Something like "Call me when the client asks for a discount bigger than 10%" is a good example of a note that you should add as a hidden note. OpenOffice.org Calc lets you add notes to any cell. It's really simple.

- Choose **Insert ➤ Comments**, which opens a yellow rectangular box where you can type short comments regarding that particular cell (see Figure 1-9).

- A cell with a note has a tiny red square in the top-right corner.

- When you want to see the note attached to a cell, right-click on the cell with the note and select **Show Comment**.

- Switching to the note editing mode is simply a matter of clicking on it when it is visible on the screen.

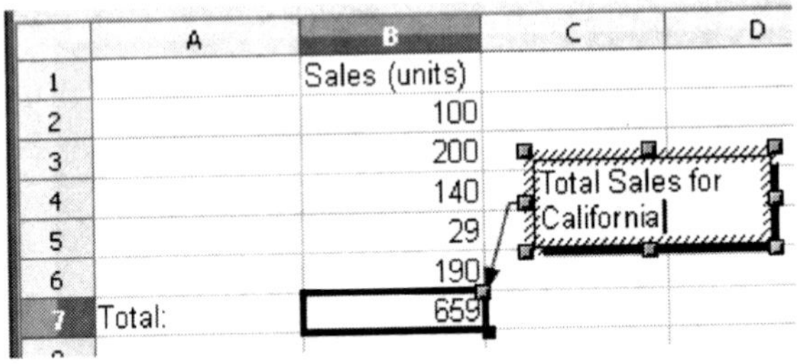

Figure 1-9. The OpenOffice.org Calc version of the famous yellow sticky notes

To delete the note, right-click on the cell with the note and choose **Delete Comment**.

CHAPTER 2

Formulas

In this chapter, you are going to learn how to write OpenOffice.org Calc formulas. Formulas are simple, yet powerful tools that let you create smart documents that automatically update themselves without too much human intervention. This may sound like rocket science, but it's actually very simple.

Once you understand how formulas works, it really is a great joy to be able to build a complex document that does all the math for you while you focus on solving the real problem.

Great Formulas

No matter what it does, every formula starts with the equal sign (=). A formula can be as simple as a reference to another cell; for example, =**A4** placed in any cell other than A4 copies the value of A4 into that cell.

Formulas can be even simpler. For example, =**7** is a formula too! But it is not very useful.

Understanding Formula Syntax

OpenOffice.org Calc formulas look and behave a lot like the equations you learned in your math classes, only the equal sign (=) is on the left hand side of the equation, rather than on the more "natural" right hand side.

All of the standard mathematical operators are available for your perusal, and they look and work just as in any other spreadsheet or math software. Their names and symbols are as follows:

- Addition (**+**)

- Subtraction (**–**)

- Multiplication (*****)

- Division (**/**)

- Exponentiation (**^**)

OpenOffice.org Calc follows the standard mathematical order of operations: exponentiation, multiplication, and division (from left to right), and addition and subtraction (from left to right).

You can change the order of formula evaluation using parentheses as shown in the following examples:

`=7+9*2^2`

returns **43**, while

`=7+(9*2)^2`

returns **331**, and

`=(7+9)*2^2`

returns **64**.

All parentheses must be matched—that is, any left parenthesis (must be matched by an appropriately placed right parenthesis).

Referencing Cells

Typing all sorts of information into a worksheet is a good way to organize it, but that is all you can do with it. If you want to process that data, you need a way to reference the values stored inside cells and a notation that lets you express how you want to process those values.

Referencing cells and processing data is possible thanks to two powerful tools: **cell addressing** and **formulas**.

- Being able to reference other cells using their addresses lets you create formulas that update their results as soon as you finish editing the values to which they refer.

- Any address inside a single sheet in a worksheet is made of two coordinates: a column number represented by a sequence of letters (e.g., **AF**) and an integer row number (e.g., **125**). Row numbers follow column numbers (e.g., **AF125**).

- A formula always begins with the equal sign (=) and can contain complex calculations described using a mixture of mathematical operators and OpenOffice.org Calc's built-in functions.

- You can use references to other cells as the arguments of OpenOffice.org Calc's functions.

The best way to see how addressing, references, and formulas work in practice is by trying out a simple example (see Figure 2-1):

Figure 2-1. *How addressing and references work in practice*
Cell A1 stores number 100; cell B1 stores the formula that references the contents of cell A1.

1. Type any number or text into any cell and remember its address.

   OpenOffice.org Calc displays the current cell's address on the toolbar in the drop-down box on the left. Column and row headers also change their color to give you visual cues.

2. Move the spreadsheet cursor to another cell.

3. Type the equal sign (=) followed by the original cell's address.

4. Press **Enter/Return**.

■ **Note** OpenOffice.org Calc displays the same numeric values or text in both cells, even though they contain different kinds of information. The first cell contains raw information, while the second contains a reference to the first cell's contents.

Relative Addressing

The type of addressing used in the example in the previous section is called "relative," because of the way OpenOffice.org Calc treats such addresses when you decide to copy or move the cells.

When you use relative addressing, OpenOffice.org Calc will update the references to point to the cells located within the same relative distance ("two cells to the left, one cell up") to the relocated cells. How does it work in practice? Suppose you have a simple formula like =A1 in cell B1. When you copy that formula from cell B1 to C1, OpenOffice.org Calc will automatically change it from =A1 to =B1.

Any time you see an address made up of letters and digits only (e.g., **A1**), it is a relative address.

Absolute Addressing

OpenOffice.org Calc is smart, but it is not smart enough to guess when you'd rather not be using relative addressing. Automatic updates of addresses used in formulas are convenient, but not always welcome.

If you don't keep an eye on what is going on, relative addressing can lead to "unexplained" errors in calculations. For example, if you enter a number into cell A4, another number into A5, and a reference to A4 (**=A4**) into cell B4 and then copy the contents of B4 into B5, B5 displays the value of A5 instead of the value of A4. Depending on your needs, this might be good or bad. If you refer to a currency exchange table, you wouldn't necessarily want to switch from one currency to another. In such cases, you should use the "absolute" addressing notation. It bolts down cell references and tells OpenOffice.org Calc to leave them the way they are.

To make sure that OpenOffice.org Calc leaves some addresses alone, put a dollar sign ($) in front of the column and the row parts of a cell's address. So, instead of typing **A4**, type **A4**. Once you do that, no matter where you copy your formula to, it will always point to the right cell.

You can use partial absolute addressing, such as **A$4** or **$A4**, to limit absolute addressing to a particular column or row, if that's what you need.

There is an easy way to change addresses from absolute to relative and back again. Select the cell in which you want to convert addresses and press **Shift+F4**. Pressing those keys repeatedly cycles through absolute rows and absolute columns, and relative rows and columns.

Referencing Data Stored on Other Sheets

You can write formulas that point to cells located on other sheets within the same worksheet document. All that you need to do is a small change of the target cell's address.

If you want to reference cell **B2** on sheet **California**, type =**California.B2**.

Referencing Data Stored in Other Worksheets

When you are referencing data held in other worksheets (separate spreadsheet document files), OpenOffice.org Calc needs some additional information to locate external files.

When you reference cell **B2** located on sheet **California** in worksheet **USA**, you need to type

```
='USA.ods'#$California.B2
```

The **.ods** suffix is used to complete the name of a worksheet created using OpenOffice.org Calc 3.1; other spreadsheets use different suffixes or no suffixes at all and you will have to adjust your references accordingly.

The pound sign (**#**) and the dollar sign (**$**) in front of the name of the sheet are obligatory. They have no relation to absolute and relative addressing, although you can use both types of addressing in cell references, such as

```
='USA.ods'#$California.$B$2
```

Filenames must be enclosed in single quotes (').

If the worksheet you are referring to is not located in the same directory as the file that references it, you must give OpenOffice.org Calc a full path to that document, such as

```
'/home/jack.white/monthly returns/customers/USA.sdc'#$California.$B$2
```

The reference to the external file shown above is written in the style native to Linux and other Unix-like operating systems. On Microsoft Windows, it would look like this:

```
='C:\Documents and Settings\Jack White\My Documents\monthly
returns\customers\USA.sdc'#$California.B2
```

Referencing Data Stored on Other Computers

You can also refer to external documents stored on the intranet or the world-wide web. To do this, choose Insert ➤ Link to External Data…

Giving Cells Names

Although addresses are a very powerful mechanism for writing formulas, they are difficult to remember. Luckily, there is a way to make your life easier. OpenOffice.org Calc lets you name each cell or whole groups of cells and use those names instead of addresses. This is how you go about doing it:

1. Select the cell you want to name.

2. Choose Insert ➤ Names ➤ Define.

3. Type the cell name (such as **Total**) into the **Name** field in the **Define Names** dialog box (see Figure 2-2).

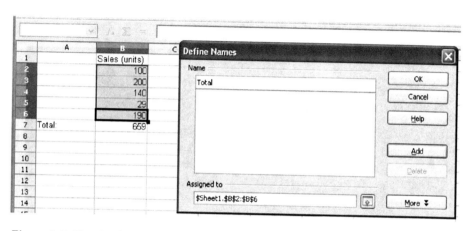

Figure 2-2. *Naming blocks of cells*

4. The names must begin with a letter and should not contain spaces, and they must be unique to distinguish them from other names.

    The **Refers to** field contains the absolute address of the cell.

5. Click on the **Add** button. That's it! You can now use the new name instead of the cell's address (e.g., use =**Total** instead of =**A1**).

You can just as easily create names for blocks of cells. Simply select as many as you like and repeat the preceding steps.

To select any cell or a range of cells that has a defined name, select the name from the list in the top-left corner of the worksheet window (see Figure 2-3).

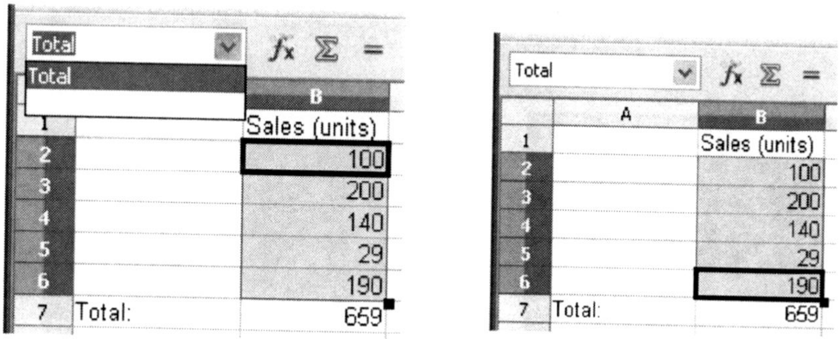

Figure 2-3. *Selecting groups of named cells*

There is another method of creating names for blocks of cells if you already have labels above, below, to the left, or to the right of each column or row of data:

1. Select cells (as in Figure 2-3) and choose Insert ➤ Names ➤ Create.

2. In the **Create Names** dialog box, click one of the options to specify the location of the labels you want to use (Figure 2-4).

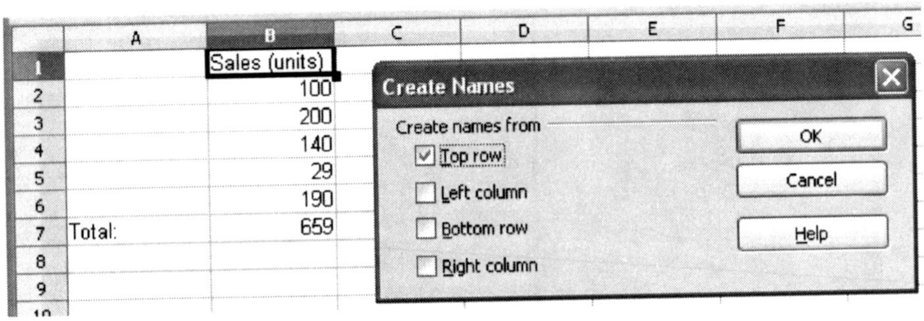

Figure 2-4. The cells you select for automatic naming must already have column or row labels.

3. Click **OK** to turn the labels into cell names.

Check if OpenOffice.org Calc did its job right by selecting one of the names from the drop-down list on the left side of the document window (see Figure 2-3).

CHAPTER 3

Functions

You might have heard that functions and formulas are difficult to master. That used to be the case a long time ago, but it is not so anymore, and it is certainly not the case with OpenOffice.org Calc.

There is some jargon to explain, but it's not difficult. As you will learn on the following pages, I often use phrases such as "the formula returns x" or "the function returns x," which is just a short way of saying that the formula or the function in question has a value of **x** for the given "parameters" or "arguments," as they are called by the creators of OpenOffice.org Calc.

What is the difference between a formula and a function? A formula is something you create yourself, using standard mathematical operators, numbers, text, cell addresses, or cell ranges. You can also add functions to a formula. Functions are really just prepackaged formulas that perform certain standardized jobs or calculations or even make simple decisions.

To use a function in a formula, you need to type its name followed by parentheses. For example, the following formula uses function **SQRT** to calculate the square root of **2**:

=SQRT(2)

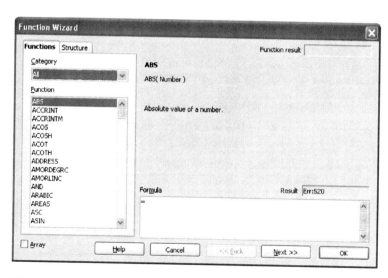

*Figure 3-1. The **Function Wizard** showing general information about functions*

The number **2** in the formula shown on the previous page is an example of a formula *argument* that a particular function accepts and processes to produce a result, which is then considered to be the value of the cell in which the formula is held.

You do not have to type function names in capitals because OpenOffice.org Calc automatically corrects them for you.

Arguments in a formula are separated by the semicolon (;).

Different functions use different arguments: numbers, text, a reference to a cell that holds a number or a text string, or another function that returns a number or a piece of text.

Using one function as an argument of another is called *nesting*. For example, you can place function **PI** inside function **SQRT**, as in

```
=SQRT(PI())
```

The example above shows function **PI** nested inside function **SQRT**.

All functions must be followed by parentheses, even if they do not take any arguments. For example, **PI()** returns the number pi (π) and doesn't take any arguments but still needs to be followed by parentheses.

In this book, we do not put parentheses after function names to make the text easier to read and to keep in line with the conventions used by the creators of OpenOffice.org Calc. The only exception is when we include actual formula code, as in =**PI()**.

Creating Formulas by Hand

Creating formulas is as simple as typing the equal sign (=) followed by the necessary references, numbers, operators, and functions into the chosen cell and then hitting the **Enter/Return** key.

If you make mistakes in the formula, OpenOffice.org Calc complains and you can edit the formula directly inside the offending cell or on the **Input Line**. All you need to do is to place the cursor in the appropriate cell and hit **F2**.

Taming the Function Wizard

There is a better, more convenient, and less error-prone way to build formulas than by typing them into a sheet. It is called the **Function Wizard**, and it serves either as an intelligent formula editor or as a handy calculator. The wizard is shown in Figure 3-1.

Here is an exercise to help you master the **Function Wizard**:

1. Click the **Function Wizard** button on the **Spreadsheet** toolbar (it looks like the letters fx)

2. Choose a formula category, such as **Financial**, from the **Category** drop-down list on the **Functions** tab. You have the following categories to choose from:

   - **Last Used**: OpenOffice.org Calc remembers which functions you used recently so you don't have to hunt for them over and over again.

   - **All**: a long list of all 300+ functions available in OpenOffice.org Calc.

- **Database**: database-like functions that operate on data arranged in rows. You can use them to write formulas that process large amount of data in a way similar to a database.

- **Date&Time**: functions for processing date and time values.

- **Financial**: financial functions.

- **Information**: information functions that provide additional information about formula results.

- **Logical**: basic logical functions.

- **Mathematical**: various math functions.

- **Array**: array/matrix processing functions.

- **Statistical**: statistical functions.

- **Spreadsheet**: spreadsheet information functions.

- **Text**: text processing functions.

- **Add-in**: additional statistical/programmers' functions.

3. Click the name of the function you want, such as **EFFECTIVE**. A short description of that function appears on the right-hand side panel.

4. Double-click the name of the chosen function. The right-hand side panel changes into a fill-in-the-blank form, with fields for every argument.

5. Enter function arguments into appropriate fields. Try entering **10%** into the **NOM** field and **12** into the **P** field. The **Function result** box in the top-right corner of the **Function Wizard** dialog box displays the value of that function. In the **Formula** field, you see the actual formula that OpenOffice.org Calc wrote while you were filling in the form fields. See Figure 3-2 to see how your formula should look.

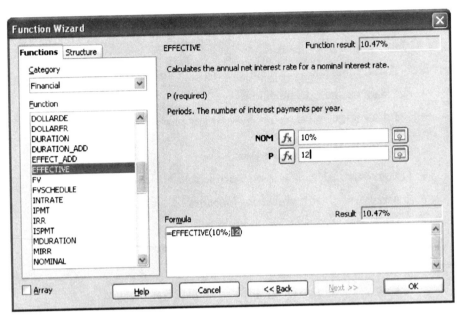

Figure 3-2. *Fill-in-the-blanks forms make designing formulas much easier than doing the work by hand.*

6. Click **OK**.

That's it. You have created a new formula now, without worrying too much about syntax rules and matching parentheses!

The tiny **Array** option box in the bottom-left corner of the **Function Wizard** dialog box is automatically marked with a tick when the result of a function is a matrix. You do not have to turn it on or off yourself unless you want to specifically stop OpenOffice.org Calc from inserting results as a matrix.

Constructing Complex Formulas

The **Function Wizard** can be used to build some really complex formulas. Try this exercise to see what it can do. We are going to create a function that reads the current date (year, month, day), adds one to the year number, and returns the day of the week for that future date:

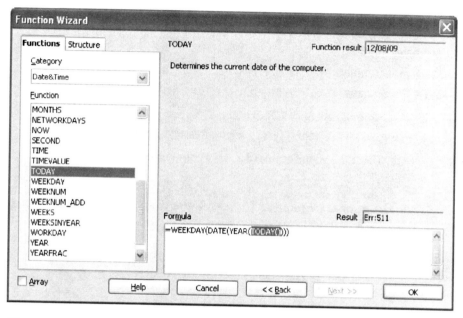

Figure 3-3. When you want to use another function as an argument, place the text cursor inside the original function's parentheses and choose the new function from the list.

1. Open the OpenOffice.org Calc **Function Wizard**.

2. Select **Date&Time** from the **Category** list.

3. Double-click the **WEEKDAY** function on the **Function** list. The right-hand side panel changes into a fill-in-the-blanks form, with fields for every argument of that function.

4. Place the mouse pointer over the parentheses after the **WEEKDAY** function displayed in the **Formula** field and click. Make sure that the text cursor is inside the parentheses.

5. Choose the **DATE** function from the **Function** list on the left and double-click it.

6. Place the mouse pointer over the parentheses after the **DATE** function displayed in the **Formula** field and click. Make sure that the text cursor is inside the parentheses.

7. Choose the **YEAR** function from the list of functions on the left and double-click it.

8. Place the text cursor inside the **YEAR** function's parentheses and choose the **TODAY** function, as shown in Figure 3-3.

9. Place the text cursor after the **YEAR(TODAY())** part of the formula and type **+1**.

10. Place the text cursor after the **(YEAR(TODAY())+1)** part of the formula and type the semicolon sign (;). You have entered the first argument of a rather complex function.

11. Using the techniques described previously, create the following formula:

    `DATE((YEAR(TODAY())+1); MONTH(TODAY()); DAY(TODAY()))`

12. The whole formula ought to look like this:

    `=WEEKDAY(DATE((YEAR(TODAY())+1); MONTH(TODAY()); DAY(TODAY())))`

13. Click **OK**. That's it. You have created a really complex formula, and it wasn't too bad, was it?

If you get lost, you might want to use the **Structure** tab in the **Function Wizard** dialog box, which visually displays the structure of the formulas you are creating (see Figure 3-4). If there are serious errors, it shows them as red spots on the list.

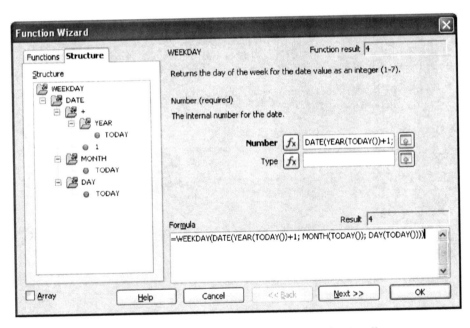

Figure 3-4. When you're lost, check the structure of the formula visually.

You can use the **Function Wizard** to do calculations without entering them into a sheet. Just compose the formula and enter appropriate values, but do not click **OK**. The results for the whole formula are shown in the **Result** box above the **Formula** field.

Formatting

OpenOffice.org Calc offers advanced data and document formatting tools. You can format sheets, cells, dates, time, numbers, text, charts, and many other objects. You can change fonts, colors, alignment, numeric formats, and anything in between and beyond. The number of available tweaks can be at times overwhelming, which is why the most popular formatting actions are located on the main toolbar (see Figure 4-1). We'll go through all formatting tools in this chapter and teach you how to use each one.

Figure 4-1. Cell formatting tools

Formatting Text

Formatting cells and sheets in the OpenOffice.org Calc worksheets is as easy as using a word processor to prettify your CV. The layout of the documents may be different because you store smaller pieces of information in tiny cells instead of putting it all in paragraphs on a long, blank page, but the general concepts are familiar.

When it comes to formatting, the only major difference between spreadsheets and word processors is the refined control you get over formatting numbers.

The Formatting Toolbar

The most popular formatting content and document tools can be found on the **Formatting** toolbar (see Table 4-1). We will discuss formatting in detail in the following sections.

Table 4-1. *Popular Cell Formatting Tools Can Be Found on the* **Formatting** *Toolbar.*

Formatting Action	Icon
Display the Styles and Formatting dialog	
Font Name list	Arial
Font Size list	10
Bold	B
Italics	I
Underline	U
Align Left	
Align Center Horizontally	
Align Right	
Justified	
Merge Cells	
Number Format: Currency	
Number Format: Percent	
Number Format: Standard	
Number Format: Add Decimal Place	
Number Format: Delete Decimal Place	
Decrease Indent	
Increase Indent	
Borders	
Background Color	
Font Color	

Cell Content Alignment

The text you enter into a cell will be treated as if it was handled by a word processor on a tiny page. That's OK, it's not like you will be using OpenOffice.org Calc to write the next *War and Peace*.

OpenOffice.org Calc will align text to the left and numbers to the right by default. You can change text alignment using four buttons: **Align Left**, **Align Center Horizontally**, **Align Right**, **Justified** (see Table 4-1).

Alternatively, you can use the following handy keyboard shortcuts:

- **Left (Ctrl+L)**: align to the left.

- **Center (Ctrl+E)**: center.

- **Justify (Ctrl+J)**: justify.

- **Right (Ctrl+R)**: align to the right.

Content alignment tools will align all types of content, not just text and numbers.

If you want to have even more alignment options, right click on the cell you want to boss around or press **Ctrl+1** and click on the **Alignment** tab (see Figure 4-2).

The tools on that tab duplicate most of the **Formatting** toolbar's functionality, but add nine additional tools that control text orientation, vertical alignment, wrapping, etc.

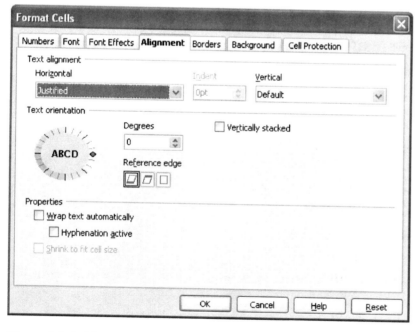

Figure 4-2. *A rich set of content alignments tools can be found on the Alignment tab* **Format Cells** *dialog.*

Here are the additional cell content adjustment options:

- **Text alignment** (Horizontal): horizontal alignment: left, right, center, justified, filled.

- **Text alignment** (Indent): paragraph indentation (activated when the horizontal alignment is set to left).

- **Text alignment** (Vertical): vertical alignment (top, middle, bottom).

- **Text orientation** (Degrees): the angle of rotation.

- **Text orientation** (Reference edge): the reference edge for rotation.

- **Text orientation** (Vertically stacked): text arranged vertically, but not rotated.

- **Properties** (Wrap text automatically): turn automatic text wrap on/off. When off, the contents longer than the cell's width will not overflow the cell's edges.

- **Properties** (Hyphenation active): turn text hyphenation on/off.

- **Properties** (Shrink to fit cell size): activated when you use rotation.

Text Styling

Once you sort out content alignment you may want to adjust the styling of text and numbers. Just like content adjustment settings, the most popular styling options have quick access buttons on the **Formatting** toolbar. These are: **Font Name**, **Font Size**, **Bold**, **Italics**, and **Underline** (see Table 4-1). They let you change fonts and font size and switch between three common type styles.

Using beautiful, expensive fonts can make your documents look professional no matter how bad the numbers presented, but try to resist the temptation to do so if those documents are going to be shared with others. The people you are going to share your files with are most likely not going to have a copy of *066.FONT's Crazy David No 1*.

Always use the standard Arial, Verdana, Georgia, and Times fonts for the best choice for smooth portability as those fonts are available on Linux, Mac OS X, and Microsoft Windows.

If you don't like clicking on buttons, here are useful keyboard shortcuts:

- **Bold (Ctrl+B)**: switch to **bold**.

- **Italics (Ctrl+I)**: switch to *italics*.

- **Underline (Ctrl+U)**: switch to <u>underline</u>.

- **Remove all formatting (Ctrl+M)**.

When you can't accomplish the desired results using the tools found on the **Formatting** toolbar, use the **Format Cells** dialog box (see Figure 4-3).

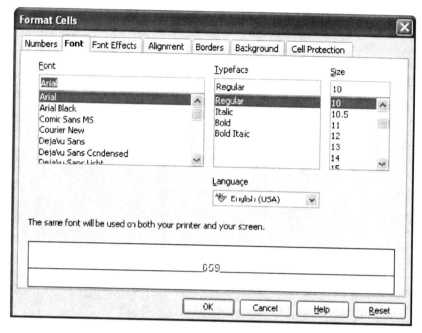

Figure 4-3. The Font formatting options available in the **Format Cells** dialog

The **Font** tab duplicates the text formatting functionality found on the **Formatting** toolbar and wouldn't be of much interest if it wasn't for the **Language** drop-down menu that lets you specify the language the text stored inside the selected cells is written in.

Although it is not immediately obvious, the language setting affects the spelling procedures, which is especially beneficial for the user speaking languages that have different local "flavors," such as U.K. English and U.S. English, as well as for those who need to create multi-language documents.

Another use for the **Fonts** tab is font preview, the box in the lower part of the **Format Cells** dialog.

To dismiss the **Format Cells** dialog, press **Esc** or click on the **Cancel** button.

Numeric Formats

Internally, OpenOffice.org Calc doesn't make any distinction between different kinds of numbers. No matter what numeric data you enter into your worksheet, if it looks like a number, it will be stored as a number. How they appear to our eyes is decided using a set of rules called numeric formats.

Quick formatting of numbers can be done when you are entering them or afterwards using the numeric formatting buttons on the **Formatting** toolbar (see Table 4-1). But if you need more, there is a list of formats available on the **Numbers** tab in the **Format Cells** dialog box (choose Format ➤ Cells or right-click the selected cell or cells and choose **Format Cells** from the pop-up menu).

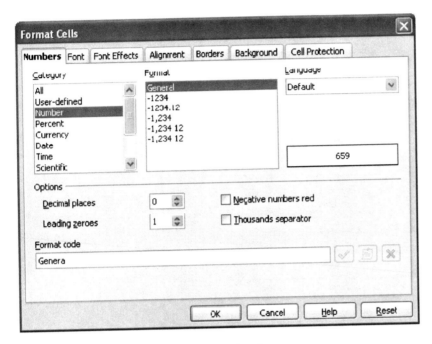

Figure 4-4. How would you like your numbers?

OpenOffice.org Calc offers literally dozens of predefined numeric formats grouped into ten categories: **User-defined, Number, Percent, Currency, Date, Time, Scientific, Fraction, Boolean Value,** and **Text.** Simply choose the category that closely matches the kind of information you want to enter into the sheet and click OK.

If you see a format that is almost, but not quite, the one you like, choose it and modify in the **Options** section of the **Format Cells** dialog box. Also, when you prepare documents in foreign languages, it is possible to choose the language used for text in dates (names of days, months) and time (AM, PM).

The display precision is controlled by the **Decimal places** scroll box. Internally, the numbers are processed with maximum possible precision.

The numeric formats are independent of the text styles applied to them. Any cell can be assigned any combination of numeric formats and text styles (font, alignment, etc.).

Type of data	Syntax
the dollar sign	$
name of a currency	CCC
a digit	#
a thousands separator	, (comma)
decimal point or period (in dates)	. (period)
percent sign	%
ordinary fraction	?/?
exponential part	E or e
date separator	/ or -
time separator	:
color used in conditional formatting	[name]
day number (without leading zeros)	D
day number (with leading zeros)	DD
short name of a day	DDD or NNN
full name of a day	DDDD
full name of a day followed by a comma	NNNN
month number (without leading zeroes)	M
month number (with leading zeroes)	MM
short name of a month	MMM
full name of a month	MMMM
a two-digit year number	YY
a four-digit year number	YYYY
the short name of a calendar quarter	Q
the name of a calendar quarter	QQ
a two-digit week number	WW

Figure 4-5. *The Conditional Formatting dialog box*

Creating Your Own Numeric Formats

Not enough numeric formats? Create your own! It is easy, although by no means as intuitive as other activities in OpenOffice.org Calc.

The best strategy is to start with the format that closely resembles the one you are trying to create and then modify it in the **Format code** input box. For example, you might like to create a format that displays money in green (when greater than zero) or red (when less than zero). Here is how you go about doing it:

1. Place the spreadsheet cursor in the chosen cell.

2. Choose Format ➤ Cells.

3. In the **Format Cells** dialog box, choose category **Currency**.

4. Choose format **-$1,234.00**.

5. Click the format code at the bottom of the dialog box and add **[GREEN]** at the beginning.

6. Click the green check mark button to add your new style (it will be listed in the **User-defined** category) and the yellow comment button to add comments, which are then displayed under the **Format** code box in the **Numbers** tab. When you look closely at the various formats' codes, you will notice that they use some special commands (see Figure 4-5).

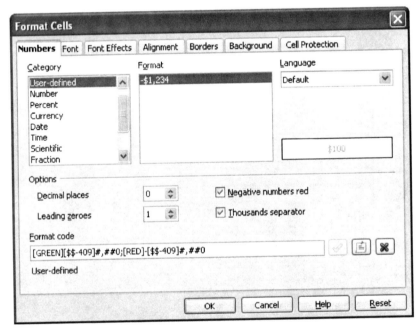

Figure 4-6. Your first custom numeric format

Creating Conditional Formatting

Conditional formatting is one of those brilliant ideas that make your work a little bit easier and more enjoyable. Conditional formatting is a great help if you want to test several choices. For example, if you are a salesperson or a manager, you might want to test several scenarios during negotiations.

It is not always to your advantage to reveal exact numbers, and this is when conditional formatting can help. It changes the style of one or more cells according to the preset conditions, which remain unseen to other people. Having visual cues is a great thing during negotiations; you know it is OK to give the discount the client asks for when you see black or green, and you know that what the client is asking for impossible when you see red.

Each cell can have up to three conditions, based on the value stored inside the cell, the value of a formula stored inside that cell, or the value of another cell that the current cell refers to.

To set these conditions, choose Format ➤ Conditional Formatting and enter the numbers into the condition boxes, as shown in Figure 4-7. After you do that, choose a different style for each condition and click **OK**. Next, type several numbers that belong to the ranges you just defined into that cell and see them displayed in different styles.

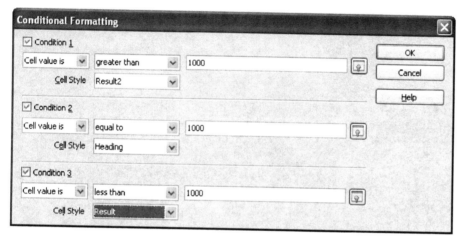

Figure 4-7. Setting up conditional formatting

The default cell styles are not very useful; therefore you need to create them, one at a time, and import them into the **Styles and Formatting** manager (press **F11**). After that, they are available in the **Conditional Formatting** dialog box.

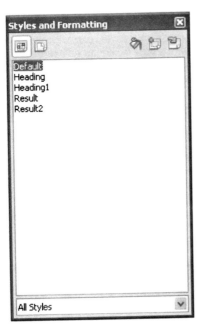

*Figure 4-8. The **Styles and Formatting** manager*

The easiest way to go about creating styles is just to follow the advice presented in the previous sections of this chapter and experiment until you are happy with how your data looks. Then, simply select the cell whose style you'd like to preserve, press F11, and click on the **New Style from Selection** button (it has a tiny green plus sign) and give it a name.

Even more advanced conditional formatting can be achieved through the use of the OpenOffice.org Calc's built-in functions, such as **STYLE**, which can change the style of a cell or a range of cells according to certain conditions set by the user.

Formatting Cells

Formatting cells (not the contents stored inside them) is done almost purely to emphasize certain facts presented on a sheet. From the designer's point of view, a cell consists of the following elements:

- **Background color**—This can be set with the **Background** button on the **Formatting** toolbar or by choosing Format ➤ Cell, clicking the **Background** tab in the **Format Cells** dialog box, and selecting the right color.

- **Borders**—These have their own tab (**Borders**) in the **Format Cells** dialog box and can be set to any color from the available list. Also, you can add shadows when you want to make something really stand out of the crowd.

Formatting Columns and Rows

Formatting columns and rows is limited to changing their width or height, hiding or showing them, and automatically choosing their optimal width or height. All of these can be performed using the Format ➤ Column or Format ➤ Row submenu.

You can also change width and height by placing the mouse pointer between the buttons with column (or row) numbers and dragging the boundary lines until they look the way you want them to.

Even better, OpenOffice.org Calc can automatically adjust column width and row height. Just place the mouse pointer between the separator buttons and double-click.

Formatting Worksheets

Formatting a worksheet is the top-most level of document design. Here you create the final layout of your work on paper and can specify the size of paper used for printing, headers, footers, page numbers, and so on.

You can't design separate layouts for individual sheets, but that is not a big problem, because you can use separate worksheets if you need different layouts.

The main page layout options are available in the **Page Style** dialog box shown in Figure 4-9.

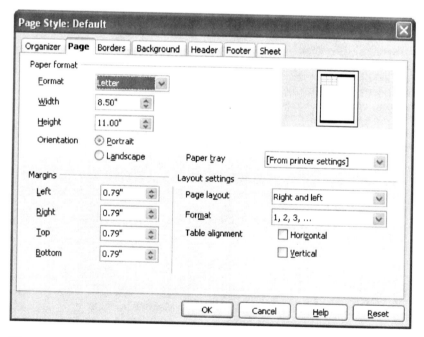

*Figure 4-9. The **Page Style** dialog box manages the final look of the printed pages.*

Choose Format ➤ Page to display the **Page Style** dialog box. There are seven tabs in this dialog box:

- **Organizer**—Enables you to choose one of the page styles available for this sheet.

- **Page**—You can set **Margins** (useful when your printer seems to chop off parts of the printout), **Paper Format** (paper size, page orientation, and paper source), which you need to specify to make your printer use the right paper, if you have more than one source; otherwise use **Printer** settings, and **Orientation**, which should really be called **Alignment** of cells on paper—click the options and see the preview box to check the results.

- **Borders**—Here you can set the borders for the page.

- **Background**—Similar to formatting cells, you can set the page background color. It is advisable that you do not use any color for printing (**No fill**) even if you have a color printer, because it is very expensive to print pages with color background. Use it only if you are printing final versions of promotional materials.

- **Header**—Here you can specify what, if anything, is to be printed at the top of each page. Also, headers can have their own borders and background; click **More** to edit these properties. If you want to edit the content of the header itself, click **Edit**. You can have separate headers for left and right pages, if you print on both sides of paper. To use them, deselect the **Same content left/right** option.

- **Footer**—Everything that applies to headers also applies to footers.

- **Sheet**: Default values on this sheet can be left alone, unless you want to print cell notes, grid, formulas, or column and row headers (**A … IV** and **1 … 32,000**), which is not necessary in most cases. However, you might change the **Page order**, if the pages progress from left to right instead of top to bottom, and, if necessary, you can specify the maximum number of pages that may be used in printing and let OpenOffice.org Calc scale them down accordingly. Do not expect miracles, but you might be able to save one page for each 6 to 10 pages. It depends on the size of the sheet and the resolution of your printer (600 dpi is best).

Sometimes OpenOffice.org Calc breaks pages in places where you would rather they were not broken. To remedy that, place the cursor in a cell where you want to insert a page break and choose Insert ➤ Manual Break ➤ Row Break or Insert ➤ Manual Break ➤ Column Break to insert the page break either above or to the left of the cell.

Removing manual breaks is just as easy: choose Edit ➤ Remove Manual Break ➤ Row Break or Edit ➤ Remove Manual Break ➤ Column Break.

Auto-formatting Sheets

If you would like to avoid the tedious formatting of cells by hand, use pre-defined formats:

1. Enter data into a sheet in some roughly organized manner.

2. Choose Format ➤ AutoFormat.

3. Select the format you like from the list on the left (see Figure 4-10).

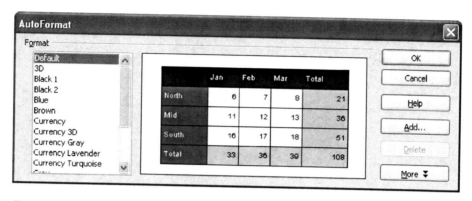

Figure 4-10. *Auto-format*

4.   Click on the **OK** button. You're done.

Adding New Designs to the Auto-format List

You can create your own sheet designs and add them to the list of formats in the **Auto-format** dialog:

1.   Enter data into a sheet in some roughly organized manner.

2.   Select the formatted area.

3.   Choose Format ➤ AutoFormat.

4.   Click the **Add...** button in the **Auto-format** dialog box.

5.   Type in the name of your new format.

6.   Click on the **OK** button. That's it!

Your new format must be at least 4 cells by 4 cells in size to be accepted by OpenOffice.org Calc.

CHAPTER 5

Simple Mathematical Functions

In this chapter, you are going to learn about popular OpenOffice.org Calc mathematical functions. It is a good idea to try the examples from this chapter to see how OpenOffice.org Calc works.

Absolute Values of Numbers (ABS)

Syntax: ABS(n)

The **ABS** function removes the minus sign (–) from a negative number, making it positive. It does nothing to **0** (zero) or positive numbers.

	A	B	C
10	**ABS**	**Number**	**Result**
11	ABS	-2	2
12	ABS	0	0
13	ABS	2	2

Figure 5-1. Sample results of the ABS function

The **ABS** function is useful if you want to further process values returned by a formula or function that may return negative results. For example:

```
=SQRT(PMT(7.5%/12; 25*12; 1,000,000))
```

produces errors because the **PMT** function (see "Calculations with Money") returns negative values for payments due. It is mathematically correct but may be confusing to some. To change that result to a positive number, use

```
=SQRT(ABS(PMT(7.5%/12; 25*12; 1,000,000)))
```

By the way, if you want to add the minus sign on every result, use

```
=-SQRT(ABS(PMT(7.5%/12; 25*12; 1,000,000)))
```

▪ **Remember** When you start wrapping functions and formulas in **ABS**, you alter their results in a way that may not be expected by other functions and formulas that rely on those results. Always think twice about the consequences of such modifications.

See also the section on the **SIGN** function.

Exponential Function (EXP)

Syntax: EXP(Number)

The EXP function returns the values of the exponential function e^x for the given number x where e is approximately equal to **2.718281828**. For example:

`=EXP(1)`

returns **2.72** (see Figure 5-2).

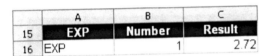

	A	B	C
15	**EXP**	**Number**	**Result**
16	EXP	1	2.72

Figure 5-2. Sample result of the EXP function

See also the sections on the **FACT, LN, LOG, LOG10, POWER**, and **SQRT** functions.

Factorial Function (FACT)

Syntax: FACT(n)

The **FACT** function returns the value of the factorial function for the given number (the product of all integers from **1** to **n**). For example:

`=FACT(3)`

returns **6** or 1 * 2 * 3.

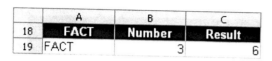

	A	B	C
18	**FACT**	**Number**	**Result**
19	FACT	3	6

Figure 5-3. Sample result of the FACT function

See also the section on the **EXP** function.

Natural Logarithm (LN)

Syntax: LN(Number)

The **LN** function returns the value of the natural logarithm (the logarithm base of e) for the given **number**. Note that the number must be positive. For example:

`=LN(8)`

returns 2.08 ($\log_e 8$).

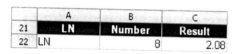

	A	B	C
21	**LN**	**Number**	**Result**
22	LN	8	2.08

Figure 5-4. Sample result of the LN function

See also the sections on the **EXP**, **LOG**, **LOG10**, and **POWER** functions.

Logarithm (LOG)

Syntax: LOG(Number; Base)

The **LOG** function returns the value of the user-defined-base logarithm for the given **number**. Note that the number must be positive. For example:

`=LOG(8; 4)`

returns **1.5** ($\log_e 4$).

	A	B	C	D
24	**LOG**	**Number**	**Base**	**Result**
25	LOG	8	2.08	2.84

Figure 5-5. *Sample result of the **LOG** function*

See also the sections on the **EXP**, **LN**, **LOG10**, and **POWER** functions.

Logarithm Base 10 (LOG10)

Syntax: LOG10(Number)

The **LOG10** function returns the value of logarithm base **10** for the given **number**. Note that the number must be positive. For example:

`=LOG10(8)`

is 0.9 ($\log_{10} 8$).

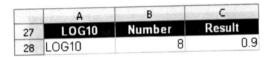

	A	B	C
27	**LOG10**	**Number**	**Result**
28	LOG10	8	0.9

Figure 5-6. *Sample result of the **LOG10** function*

See also the sections on the **EXP**, **LN**, **LOG**, and **POWER** functions.

Power (POWER)

Syntax: POWER(Number; Power)

The **POWER** function returns **number** raised to the given **power**. For example:

`=POWER(10; 2)`

returns **100**, or **102**. It is equivalent to the following notation:

`=10^2`

	A	B	C	D
30	**POWER**	**Number**	**Power**	**Result**
31	POWER	10	2	100

*Figure 5-7. Sample result of the **POWER** function*

See also the sections on the **EXP**, **FACT**, **LN**, **LOG**, **LOG10**, and **SQRT** functions.

Product of Many Arguments (PRODUCT)

Syntax: PRODUCT(ARG1; ARG2; … ARG30)

The **PRODUCT** function multiplies up to 30 arguments (**x1**, **x2**, … **x30**). Each argument can be a single value or a range of cells. For example:

`=PRODUCT(A1:A23; B2:C23)`

multiplies values of all cells from ranges **A1:A23** and **B2:C23**.

	A	B	C	D
33	**PRODUCT**	**ARG1**	**ARG2**	**ARG3**
34	PRODUCT	10	2	100
35		**ARG4**	**ARG5**	**ARG6**
36		10	2	100
37	**Result**	**ARG7**	**ARG8**	**ARG9**
38	8000000000	10	2	100

*Figure 5-8. Sample result of the **PRODUCT** function*

See also the section on the **SUM** function.

Square Root (SQRT)

Syntax: SQRT(Number)

The **SQRT** function returns the square root of a positive **number**. For example, to find a square root of 10, you'd type

`=SQRT(10)`

The answer is, of course, **3.16**.

	A	B	C
40	**SQRT**	**Number**	**Result**
41	SQRT	10	3.16

Figure 5-9. Sample result of the SQRT function

When you need to calculate the square root of a negative value, use the **ABS** function to remove the minus sign (see the description of the **ABS** function). Strictly speaking, this is not correct from a mathematical point of view, because you cannot compute a square root of a negative number, but it is perfectly acceptable when you deal with the results produced by financial functions. If you are using a method that specifically forbids this trick, you need to work with complex numbers.

OpenOffice.org Calc does provide functions for dealing with complex numbers if you need to obey the laws of mathematics. A proper discussion of complex numbers is outside of the scope of this book, but any decent college math textbook will help you understand them.

Also see the section on the **POWER** function.

Sum of Many Arguments (SUM)

Syntax: SUM(x1; x2; … x30)

The **SUM** function adds up to 30 arguments **x1**, **x2**, … **x30** and each such argument can be a range of cells. For example:

`=SUM(M1:N23; Z2:AA23)`

adds all cells from ranges **M1:N23** and **Z2:AA23**.

	A	B	C	D
43	**SUM**	**ARG1**	**ARG2**	**ARG3**
44	SUM	10	2	100
45		**ARG4**	**ARG5**	**ARG6**
46		10	2	100
47	**Result**	**ARG7**	**ARG8**	**ARG9**
48	336	10	2	100

Figure 5-10. Sample result of the SUM function

See also the section on the **PRODUCT** function.

Sum of Squares of Many Arguments (SUMSQ)

Syntax: SUMSQ(x1; x2; … x30)

The **SUMSQ** function adds squares of up to 30 arguments **x1**, **x2**, … **x30** and each such argument can be a range of cells. For example:

`=SUMSQ(M1:N23; Z2:AA23)`

adds all squares of the numeric values held in cells from ranges **M1:N23** and **Z2:AA23**.

	A	B	C	D
50	SUMSQ	ARG1	ARG2	ARG3
51	SUMSQ	10	2	100
52		ARG4	ARG5	ARG6
53		10	2	100
54	Result	ARG7	ARG8	ARG9
55	30312	10	2	100

Figure 5-11. *Sample result of the SUMSQ function*

See also the section on the **SUM** function.

CHAPTER 6

Utility Mathematical Functions

In this chapter, you will get to know useful functions that help you solve many practical problems related to crunching numbers.

Nearest Multiple Larger Than or Equal To X (CEILING)

Syntax: CEILING(Number; Significance; Mode)

The **CEILING** function rounds the given **number** up to the nearest multiple of **significance** equal to or greater than **number** itself. It is used in filtering noises out of a large number of values, spotting significant changes in values, detecting trend reversals, and similar tasks where it is easier to work with multiples of integers to get a better understanding of the sea of data you need to work with.

	A	B	C	D	E
57	CEILING	Number	Significance	Mode	Result
58	CEILING	-13	-4	1	-16
59	CEILING	-13	-4	0	-12
60	CEILING	-13	-4		-12

Figure 6-1. Sample results of the CEILING function

The **CEILING** function is also a great tool for solving mundane problems such as ordering the right amount of boxes for shipping. For example, suppose you have **125,000** unsold USB drives that you want to get rid of using that old "buy-thirteen-get-five-free" technique. Why thirteen and five? Because the cheapest boxes you could find will hold a maximum of **18** drives and you want to sound original. Here's how you use **CEILING**:

```
=CEILING(125,000; 18)
```

The result you will get is 125,010. This tells you how many USB sticks you would need to fill all boxes with exactly **18** USB drives, but you only have **125,000** USB drives. That's OK. One of the boxes will have less than **18** USB drives. You will give a special discount on those or just give them away. But you still need to know how many boxes you need. Here's how to get that number:

```
=CEILING(125,000; 18)/18
```

And the answer is **6945**.

What if those boxes are sold one dozen per package? How many packages should you order?

```
=CEILING(CEILING(125,000; 18)/18; 12)/12
```

And here is the answer: **579** packages.

You could say that **CEILING** is similar to **ROUND** or **ROUNDUP**, but that is only partially true. While the **ROUND** function will obey the math rules for rounding fractional numbers and round them up and down accordingly, **CEILING** always rounds up. The **ROUNDUP** function is closer in its behavior to **CEILING**, but it needs a little more typing; for example, you have to specify the number of decimal places for results.

The third argument in **CEILING**, **mode**, is used to specify rounding rules for negative numbers. When you omit this argument, the number is rounded up to the nearest multiple of a given negative number. For example:

```
=CEILING(-13; -2)
```

returns **–12**, which is greater than **–13**, unless you add **1** as **mode to round down**, as in

```
=CEILING(-13; -2; 1)
```

which returns **–14**.

You cannot mix negative and positive numbers. For example: CEILING(-13;2) is not allowed.

See also the sections on the **EVEN**, **FLOOR**, **INT**, **ODD**, **ROUND**, **ROUNDDOWN**, **ROUNDUP**, and **TRUNC** functions.

Nearest Even Integer (EVEN)

Syntax: EVEN(Number)

The **EVEN** function is useful when you want results to be presented as even integer numbers. It rounds the given **number** up to the nearest even integer, which is just what you need if you need to count quantities such as "pairs of socks" or "pairs of gloves." For example, if your worksheet reports that you need to sell **12,467.349888** socks to pay off the money gods, use the following formula to turn that cold number into something a human can understand:

```
=EVEN(12,467.349888)/2
```

The result will be **6234** pairs of socks, which is a much more useful and natural way to present such quantities. Of course, you do not have to put the actual number into that function; a reference to another cell that stores the value to be rounded up is as useful, as is nesting another function inside the **EVEN** function.

	A	B	C
62	**EVEN**	**Number**	**Result**
63	EVEN	13	14

Figure 6-2. Sample result of the EVEN function

See also the sections on the **CEILING, INT, FLOOR, ODD, ROUND, ROUNDDOWN,** and **ROUNDUP** functions.

Nearest Multiple Smaller Than or Equal To X (FLOOR)

Syntax: FLOOR(Number; Significance; Mode)

The **FLOOR** function rounds the given **number** down to the nearest multiple of **significance**. It is similar to **CEILING**, but instead of "padding" the given numbers, it will "shave a little off their top." For example, in the section on the **CEILING** functions you read about looking for the number of boxes needed to pack **18** USB drives given the total number of those drives and the fact that the boxes are sold in dozens. As you recall, one box will have less than 18 drives in it. You can use the **FLOOR** function to find out how many boxes you would need to buy if you wanted to have exactly 18 drives in each and keep the remainder unboxed. Here's the formula you need:

```
=FLOOR(125,000; 18)/18
```

And the answer is 6944.

	A	B	C	D	E
65	**FLOOR**	**Number**	**Significance**	**Mode**	**Result**
66	FLOOR	-13	-4	1	-12
67	FLOOR	-13	-4	0	-16
68	FLOOR	-13	-4		-16

Figure 6-3. Sample results of the FLOOR function

Negative values are rounded down to the nearest multiple of a given negative number. For example:

```
=FLOOR(-13; -2)
```

returns −14, unless you add 1 as **mode to round up**, as in

```
=FLOOR(-13; -2; 1)
```

which returns −12.

You cannot mix negative and positive numbers. For example, FLOOR(-13;2) is not allowed.

See also the sections on the **CEILING, EVEN, INT, ODD, ROUND, ROUNDDOWN, ROUNDUP,** and **TRUNC** functions.

Nearest Integer (INT)

Syntax: INT(Number)

The **INT** function rounds the given **number** down to the nearest integer. For example:

`=INT(12.3)`

returns **12**.

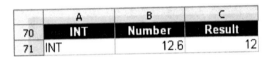

	A	B	C
70	**INT**	**Number**	**Result**
71	INT	12.6	12

Figure 6-4. Sample result of the INT function

> See also the sections on the **CEILING, EVEN, FLOOR, ODD, ROUND, ROUNDDOWN,** and **ROUNDUP** functions.

Nearest Odd Integer (ODD)

Syntax: ODD(Number)

This is the function to use if you want results to be rounded up to the nearest odd integer. For example:

`=ODD(12.3)`

returns **13**.

	A	B	C
73	**ODD**	**Number**	**Result**
74	ODD	12.6	13

Figure 6-5. Sample result of the ODD function

> See also the sections on the **CEILING, EVEN, INT, FLOOR, ROUND, ROUNDDOWN,** and **ROUNDUP** functions.

Random Number (RAND)

Syntax: RAND()

The **RAND** function returns a random fractional number between **0** and **1**. To make it a bit more useful, you can multiply it by **10** and use **TRUNC** to turn the results into integers from **0** to **10**. Here's an example:

```
=TRUNC(RAND()*10)
```

Multiplying **RAND** by **100** in the preceding example returns numbers from **0** to **100**.

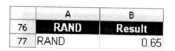

	A	B
76	**RAND**	**Result**
77	RAND	0.65

Figure 6-6. *Sample result of the RAND function*

If you want random numbers from a different range, such as **1970** to **2010**, use the following trick:

```
=TRUNC(RAND()*40)+1970
```

See also the section on the **TRUNC** function.

Rounding Numbers (ROUND)

Syntax: ROUND(x; y)

The **ROUND** function rounds **x** to **y** decimal places, as in

```
=ROUND(1.2533; 1)
```

which returns the argument rounded to one decimal place, or **1.3**.

	A	B	C	D
79	**ROUND**	**Number**	**Count**	**Result**
80	ROUND	12.6543210	3	12.6540000

Figure 6-7. *Sample result of the ROUND function*

Using **0** as the number of decimal places rounds numbers to whole integers.
See also the sections on the **CEILING, EVEN, FLOOR, INT, ODD**, and **TRUNC** functions.

Rounding Numbers Down (ROUNDDOWN)

Syntax: ROUNDDOWN(x; y)

The **ROUNDDOWN** function does exactly what you'd expect; it rounds the first argument down to the specified number of decimal places, as in

`=ROUNDDOWN(1.2533; 1)`

which returns **1.2**.

	A	B	C	D
82	**ROUNDDOWN**	**Number**	**Count**	**Result**
83	ROUNDDOWN	12.6543210	3	12.6540000

*Figure 6-8. Sample result of the **ROUNDDOWN** function*

Using **0** as the number of decimal places rounds numbers to whole integers.
See also the sections on the **CEILING**, **EVEN**, **FLOOR**, **INT**, **ODD**, and **TRUNC** functions.

Rounding Numbers Up (ROUNDUP)

Syntax: ROUNDUP(x; y)

The **ROUNDUP** function, just as you'd expect, rounds numeric values up to the specified number of decimal places, as in

`=ROUNDUP(7.111; 1)`

which returns **7.2**.
Using 0 as the number of decimal places rounds numbers to whole integers.

	A	B	C	D
85	**ROUNDUP**	**Number**	**Count**	**Result**
86	ROUNDUP	12.6543210	3	12.6550000

*Figure 6-9. Sample result of the **ROUNDUP** function*

See also the sections on the **CEILING**, **EVEN**, **FLOOR**, **INT**, **ODD**, and **TRUNC** functions.

Truncate (TRUNC)

Syntax: TRUNC(x; y)

The **TRUNC** function is different from other rounding functions. It does not round number **x**, but chops off its fractional part, leaving **y** digits after the decimal point (if the second argument is omitted, **TRUNC** chops off the whole fractional part of a number turning it into an integer). For example:

`=TRUNC(12.5)`

returns **12**. The subtle difference between **TRUNC** and **INT** is best explained when you use the same negative number as an argument for these functions; for example:

`=TRUNC(-15.72)`

returns −**15**, while

`=INT(-15.72)`

returns −**16**.
    In this example **TRUNC** is used with a second argument and

`=TRUNC(16.2371; 2)`

returns **16.23**.

	A	B	C	D
88	**TRUNC**	**Number**	**Count**	**Result**
89	TRUNC	12.6543210	3	12.6540000
90	TRUNC	12.6543210		12.0000000

*Figure 6-10. Sample results of the **TRUNC** function*

See also the sections on the **CEILING, EVEN, FLOOR, INT, ODD, ROUND, ROUNDDOWN,** and **ROUNDUP** functions.
    For more mathematical functions click the **Function Wizard** button and choose **Mathematical** or **Matrix** from the **Categories** list.

CHAPTER 7

Useful Statistical Functions

Statistical functions operate on a series or ranges of values. The examples in this chapter are simplified, but adequate for most purposes.

Average (AVERAGE)

Syntax: AVERAGE(x1; x2; … x30)

The **AVERAGE** function returns the average of up to **30** given arguments separated with the semicolon sign (;). Each such argument may be a range of cells. For example:

`=AVERAGE(12.55; 10.93; 11.78; 12.00; 11.54; 12.67; 23.56; 45.21; 0.67)`

returns **15.66**.

	A	B	C	D
92	**AVERAGE**	**ARG1**	**ARG2**	**ARG3**
93	AVERAGE	12.55	10.93	11.78
94		**ARG4**	**ARG5**	**ARG6**
95		12	11.54	12.67
96	**Result**	**ARG7**	**ARG8**	**ARG9**
97	15.66	23.56	45.21	0.67

*Figure 7-1. Sample result of the **AVERAGE** function*

Geometric Mean (GEOMEAN)

Syntax: GEOMEAN(x1; x2; … x30)

The **GEOMEAN** function returns the geometric mean of up to **30** given arguments separated with the semicolon sign (;). Each such argument may be a range of cells. For example:

=GEOMEAN(12.55; 10.93; 11.78; 12.00; 11.54; 12.67; 23.56; 45.21; 0.67)

returns **10.81**.

	A	B	C	D
92	**GEOMEAN**	**ARG1**	**ARG2**	**ARG3**
93	GEOMEAN	12.55	10.93	11.78
94		**ARG4**	**ARG5**	**ARG6**
95		12	11.54	12.67
96	**Result**	**ARG7**	**ARG8**	**ARG9**
97	10.81	23.56	45.21	0.67

Figure 7-2. Sample result of the GEOMEAN function

Harmonic Mean (HARMEAN)

Syntax: HARMEAN(x1; x2; … x30)

The **HARMEAN** function returns the harmonic mean of up to **30** given arguments separated with the semicolon sign (;). Each such argument may be a range of cells. For example:

=HARMEAN(12.55; 10.93; 11.78; 12.00; 11.54; 12.67; 23.56; 45.21; 0.67)

returns **4.36**.

	A	B	C	D
99	**HARMEAN**	**ARG1**	**ARG2**	**ARG3**
100	HARMEAN	12.55	10.93	11.78
101		**ARG4**	**ARG5**	**ARG6**
102		12	11.54	12.67
103	**Result**	**ARG7**	**ARG8**	**ARG9**
104	4.36	23.56	45.21	0.67

Figure 7-3. Sample result of the HARMEAN function

Median (MEDIAN)

Syntax: MEDIAN(x1; x2; … x30)

The MEDIAN function returns the median of up to 30 given arguments separated with the semicolon sign (;). Each such argument may be a range of cells. For example, the following function

=MEDIAN(12.55; 10.93; 11.78; 12.00; 11.54; 12.67; 23.56; 45.21; 0.67)

returns **12**.

If the number of arguments is even, then the mean of the two middle values is the median.

	A	B	C	D
106	**MEDIAN**	**ARG1**	**ARG2**	**ARG3**
107	MEDIAN	12.55	10.93	11.78
108		**ARG4**	**ARG5**	**ARG6**
109		12	11.54	12.67
110	**Result**	**ARG7**	**ARG8**	**ARG9**
111	12	23.56	45.21	0.67

Figure 7-4. Sample result of the MEDIAN function

Counting Cells (COUNT)

Syntax: COUNT(x1; x2; ... x30)

The **COUNT** function accepts a maximum of **30** separate arguments (single values and ranges of cells) and returns the number of arguments that contain numeric values. For example:

```
=COUNT("OpenOffice.org"; 7139; 12.99)
```

returns **2**.

	A	B	C	D
113	**COUNT**	**ARG1**	**ARG2**	**ARG3**
114	COUNT	12.55	10.93	c
115		**ARG4**	**ARG5**	**ARG6**
116		12	b	12.67
117	**Result**	**ARG7**	**ARG8**	**ARG9**
118	6	a	45.21	0.67

Figure 7-5. Sample result of the COUNT function

Counting Cells (COUNTA)

Syntax: COUNTA(x1; x2; ... x30)

The **COUNTA** function accepts a maximum of **30** separate arguments (single values and ranges of cells) and returns the number of arguments that contain any kind of values (empty cells are ignored). For example:

```
=COUNTA("OpenOffice.org"; 7139; 12.99)
```

returns **3**.

	A	B	C	D
120	**COUNTA**	**ARG1**	**ARG2**	**ARG3**
121	COUNTA	12.55	10.93	c
122		**ARG4**	**ARG5**	**ARG6**
123		12	b	12.67
124	**Result**	**ARG7**	**ARG8**	**ARG9**
125	9	a	45.21	0.67

Figure 7-6. Sample result of the COUNTA function

The Kth Largest Value (LARGE)

Syntax: LARGE(x; k)

The **LARGE** function returns the kth largest numeric value found in the given set of values **x**; for example, when given the set of values of **12.55**, **10.93**, and **11.78**, **LARGE** returns the following result:

```
=LARGE(B128:D128; 3)
```

returns **10.93**, which is the 3rd largest value in the given set.

	A	B	C	D
127	**LARGE**	**ARG1**	**ARG2**	**ARG3**
128	LARGE	12.55	10.93	11.78
129			**Rank**	**Result**
130			2	11.78

Figure 7-7. Sample result of the LARGE function

You can set the **k** argument to any integer value you like, but it must not be zero or larger than the number of elements in the given set of numbers.

See also the sections on the **SMALL**, **MAX**, and **MIN** functions.

The Kth Smallest Value (SMALL)

Syntax: SMALL(x; k)

The **SMALL** function returns the kth largest numeric value found in the given set of values **x**; for example, when given the set of values of **12.55**, **10.93**, and **11.78**, **SMALL** returns the following result:

```
=SMALL(B133:D133; 3)
```

returns **12.55**. which is the 3rd smallest value in the given set.

	A	B	C	D
132	**SMALL**	**ARG1**	**ARG2**	**ARG3**
133	SMALL	12.55	10.93	11.78
134			**Rank**	**Result**
135			3	12.55

Figure 7-8. *Sample result of the SMALL function*

You can set the **k** argument to any integer value you like, but it must not be zero or larger than the number of elements in the given set of numbers.

See also the sections on the **LARGE**, **MAX**, and **MIN** functions.

Maximum (MAX)

Syntax: MAX(x1; x2; … x30)

The **MAX** function can take up to **30** arguments, which can be ranges of cells, and returns the maximum value found in the given set. For example:

```
=MAX(B138; C138; D138; B140; C140; D140, B142; C142; D142)
```

results in **100**.

	A	B	C	D
137	**MAX**	**ARG1**	**ARG2**	**ARG3**
138	MAX	67	2	100
139		**ARG4**	**ARG5**	**ARG6**
140		10	23	97
141	**Result**	**ARG7**	**ARG8**	**ARG9**
142	100	32	56	99

Figure 7-9. *Sample result of the MAX function*

See also the sections on the **LARGE**, **MIN**, and **SMALL** functions.

Minimum (MIN)

Syntax: MIN(x1; x2; ... x30)

The **MAX** function can take up to **30** arguments, which can be ranges of cells, and returns the maximum value found in the given set. For example:

`=MIN(B145; C145; D145; B147; C147; D147, B149; C149; D149)`

returns **2**.

	A	B	C	D
144	MIN	ARG1	ARG2	ARG3
145	MIN	67	2	100
146		ARG4	ARG5	ARG6
147		10	23	97
148	Result	ARG7	ARG8	ARG9
149	2	32	56	99

Figure 7-10. Sample result of the MIN function

See also the sections on the **LARGE**, **MAX**, and **SMALL** functions.

Mode Function (MODE)

Syntax: MODE(x1; x2; ... x30)

The **MODE** function returns the most common value in a data set that can consist of up to 30 arguments, which can be single values or ranges of cells. You can provide up to **30** arguments. For example, if you give **MODE** the following set:

`MODE(67, 2, 100, 10, 2, 97, 32, 56, 99)`

MODE returns **2**.

	A	B	C	D
151	MODE	ARG1	ARG2	ARG3
152	MODE	67	2	100
153		ARG4	ARG5	ARG6
154		10	2	97
155	Result	ARG7	ARG8	ARG9
156	2	32	56	99

Figure 7-11. Sample result of the MODE function

See also the section on the **RANK** function.

Rank Function (RANK)

Syntax: RANK(number; set; order)

The **RANK** function returns the rank of a given number in the given set of numbers. You give it a value, a set, and **RANK** will tell you if the given number is 1st, 2nd, 3rd, and so on.

	A	B	C	D
158	**RANK**			
159				
160	**ARG1**	**ARG2**	**ARG3**	**ARG4**
161	25.00%	27.00%	15.00%	33.00%
162				
163	**Order**	**Order**		
164		1		
165				
166	**Result**	**Result**		
167	3	2		

Figure 7-12. *Sample results of the **RANK** function*

For example, if you wanted to know how your company's share of the market is determined, you'd use something like:

```
=RANK(25%; A161:D161)
```

RANK returns **3**, indicating that your company is the third largest player on the market. You can reverse the order of the ranking if you use the third argument equal to **1** (descending); **0** is ascending, but you can omit that because it is a default value. For example:

```
=RANK(25%; A1:A4; 1)
```

returns **2**, indicating that your company is the second smallest player on the market.

For more statistical functions, click the **Function Wizard** button and choose **Statistical** from the **Categories** list.

CHAPTER 8

Calculations with Money

Although OpenOffice.org Calc's mathematical and statistical functions are advanced enough to construct any financial function you might need, you don't have to do it. OpenOffice.org Calc ships with many built-in financial functions such as rates of return and future values of investments. This chapter is all about them.

The financial functions can be divided into the following groups:

- Investment calculations.

- Asset depreciation.

Investment Calculations

Investment calculation functions are used to compute interest rates, payments, and the length of time needed to repay a loan. They are also a good tool to use to compare the profitability of various investments.

Cumulative Compounded Interest (CUMIPMT)

Syntax: CUMIPMT(Interest; Time; Capital; Start; End; Type)

The **CUMIPMT** (cumulative compounded interest) function returns the amount of interest that needs to be paid on the principal or capital, borrowed for a period of time. It is defined as the total number of payment periods (months, quarters, years, and so on).

	A	B	C	D
169	CUMIPMT	INTEREST	TIME	CAPITAL
170	CUMIPMT	7.25%	25	$1,000,000
171				
172		START	END	TYPE
173		1	3	0
174				
175	Result			
176	-$18,103.45			

*Figure 8-1. Sample result of the **CUMIPMT** function*

It is assumed that the rate of interest remains constant for the whole accounting period. You can calculate the amount of interest to be paid back for the whole period or a part of it using the **start** and **end** arguments. For example, if you borrow **$1,000,000** for 25 years at a constant rate of interest of **7.25%** and want to know how much interest you need to pay in the first quarter of the first year, assuming monthly payments made at the beginning of each month, you need to use the following function:

=CUMIPMT(7.25%/12; 25*12; 1,000,000; 1; 3; 0)

The result is **–$18,103.45**.

It is necessary to divide the rate of interest and multiply the number of years by the number of months (or equivalent payment periods) to make sure that the calculations are correct. For quarterly payments the function would look like this:

=CUMIPMT(7.25%/4; 25*4; 1,000,000; 1; 1; 0)

The fourth and fifth arguments (**start** and **end**) indicate the start and end payment periods for which the amount of compound interest is being calculated.

In the first example it was the first and the third month of the first year; in the second example it was the first quarter of the first year. The first month of the second year would be represented by **13**, and the first quarter of the second year would be represented by **5**.

The last argument, **type**, is used to tell OpenOffice.org Calc when payments are made. When money is paid at the beginning of each accounting period, use **1** and when money is to be made at the end of each accounting period, use **0**.

It is a generally accepted rule that we mark arguments and results with the minus sign (–) when they indicate money that needs to be paid out to somebody and without the minus sign when the money is received. OpenOffice.org Calc's functions do it automatically for the results but not for the arguments (however, OpenOffice.org Calc returns an error if you put a minus sign where it is not supposed to be).

Also see the description of the **CUMPRINC** function, which calculates the amount of compound principal capital paid back over a given period of time.

Always remember to put the right percentage values into functions that require them. There is a big difference between **10** (which OpenOffice.org Calc interprets as **1,000%** or one thousand percent) and **10%**.

Cumulative Principal Capital (CUMPRINC)

Syntax: CUMPRINC(Interest; Time; Capital; Start; End; Type)

Complementary to the **CUMIPMT** function, **CUMPRINC** returns the amount of the compound principal capital that needs to be paid back within a given period of time defined as the total number of payment periods (months, quarters, years, and so on). It is assumed that the rate of interest remains constant for the whole accounting period.

	A	B	C	D
178	**CUMPRINC**	**INTEREST**	**TIME**	**CAPITAL**
179	CUMPRINC	7.25%	25	$1,000,000
180				
181		**START**	**END**	**TYPE**
182		1	3	0
183				
184	**Result**			
185	-$3,580.75			

Figure 8-2. *Sample result of the **CUMPRINC** function*

     This function is useful if you want to know how much of the principal capital borrowed needs to be paid back within the specified amount of time or any shorter interval specified by the **start** and **end** arguments.

     For example, if you borrow **$1,000,000** for **25** years at a constant rate of interest of **7.25%** and want to know how much capital you need to return within the first quarter of the first year (assuming monthly payments made at the beginning of each month), you need to use the following function:

```
=CUMPRINC(7.25%/12; 25*12; 1,000,000; 1; 3; 0)
```

     The result is $3,580.75. It is necessary to divide the rate of interest, and multiply the number of years, by the number of months (or equivalent payment periods) to make sure that the calculations are correct. For quarterly payments, the function would look like this:

```
=CUMPRINC7.25%/4; 25*4; 1,000,000; 1; 1; 0)
```

     The function returns **–$3,605.44**, which is more than **–$3,580.75** from the previous example.

     The fourth and fifth arguments (**start** and **end**) indicate the start and end payment periods for which the amount of compound capital is being calculated.

     In the first example it was the first and the third months of the first year; in the second example it was the first quarter of the first year. The first month of the second year would have number **13** and the first quarter of the second year would have number **5**.

     If the payments are to be made at the beginning of each accounting period, use **1** instead of **0** as the last argument (**type**) of this function.

     Also see the description of the **CUMIPMT** function, which calculates the amount of interest on principal capital to be paid back in a given amount of time.

Time to Maturity (DURATION)

Syntax: DURATION(Interest; Investment; Future)

The **DURATION** function returns the number of periods (years if a yearly interest rate is used) for a given investment to reach the desired future value, assuming a constant rate of interest. For example, if you want to know how many years you have to wait for **$1,000** deposited in a bank account that pays **3%** interest annually for your money to become **$2,000**, use the following formula:

```
=DURATION(3%; 1000; 2000)
```

	A	B	C	D	E
187	**DURATION**	**Interest**	**Investment**	**Future**	**Result**
188	DURATION	3.00%	$1,000.00	$2,000.00	23.45

*Figure 8-3. Sample result of the **DURATION** function*

The answer is a long **23.45** years. If you want to see the answer given in whole years, without fractions, use the **ROUNDUP** function, as in

```
=ROUNDUP(DURATION(3%; 1000; 2000); 0)
```

Effective Rate of Interest (EFFECTIVE)

Syntax: EFFECTIVE(Nominal; Periods)

The **EFFECTIVE** function returns the effective annual rate of interest for the nominal rate of interest and the number of payment periods (typically months if the nominal rate is an annual rate). So, if you want to check the effective rate of interest for a nominal rate of **10%**, assuming **12** monthly payments, use

```
=EFFECTIVE(10%; 12)
```

This returns **10.47%**.

	A	B	C	D
190	**EFFECTIVE**	**Nominal**	**Periods**	**Result**
191	EFFECTIVE	10.00%	12	10.47%

*Figure 8-4. Sample result of the **EFFECTIVE** function*

The opposite of this function is **NOMINAL.**

Future Value (FV)

Syntax: FV(Interest; Time; Installment; Deposit; Type)

The **FV** function returns the future value of an initial lump **deposit** investment followed by the given number of regular, equal installments made over a length of **time**, assuming a constant rate of **interest**.

	A	B	C	D
193	FV	Interest	Time	Installment
194	FV	5.00%	25	-$100.00
195				
196		Deposit	Type	
197		-$10,000.00	0	
198				
199	Result			
200	$94,363.88			

Figure 8-5. *Sample result of the **FV** function*

The **time** argument specifies the total number of payments, and the **installment** argument is the amount of money paid each time.

For example, if you want to know how much money you could save if you paid **$100** each month for **25** years into a savings account that pays a constant interest of **5%**, you could use the following formula:

```
=FV(5%/12; 25*12; -100)
```

The answer is **$59,550.97**. Not bad at all, but how much could you save if you paid **$1,200** annually? Let's see:

```
=FV(5%; 25; -1,200)
```

returns **$57,272.52**.

Clearly, it is more profitable to pay in smaller amounts but more frequently.

Remember that the rate of **interest** ought to be followed by the percentage (**%**) sign and, for payments made more frequently than once per year, the rate of interest must be divided by the number of payments in a year. For monthly payments it means that the rate of interest is divided by **12**, for quarterly payments the rate of interest is divided by **4**, and so on.

The **time** argument must be equal to the number of payments made. For example, for an investment in which contributions are made monthly for four years, you'd make time equal to **48** (**4*12**).

In both of the previous calculations we assumed that you made deposits at the beginning of the accounting period. To calculate payments at the end of the accounting period, you need to use the fifth argument type, which can be set to **0** for payments made at the end of each accounting period. Use **1** for payments made at the beginning of each accounting period. If you use the fifth argument, you must also enter the fourth, **deposit**, as well, which is used to give the initial amount of savings.

The **FV** function may be used for some more complex calculations. You might want to know, for example, how much your current savings, say **$10,000**, will be worth in **25** years if you boost it with monthly payments of **$100**. Here you go:

```
=FV(5%/12; 25*12; -100; -10,000; 0)
```

The answer is a healthy **$94,363.88** (payments made at the end of each accounting period) compared to an even nicer **$94,612.00** when payments are made at the beginning of each accounting period.

It is necessary to divide the rate of interest, and multiply the number of years, by the number of months (or equivalent payment periods) to make sure that the calculations are correct. The rate of interest is always assumed to be the annual rate of interest. Therefore, if you need to compute monthly payments, you need to divide the rate by **12** and multiply the number of years by **12**. Similarly, if you were computing quarterly payments, you would divide the interest rate by 4 and multiply the number of years by 4.

See also the description of the **PV** function.

Interest (IPMT)

Syntax: IPMT(Interest; Period; Time; Loan; Future; Type)

The **IPMT** function returns the amount of interest that you need to pay in a given accounting **period** when you borrow a certain amount of money (**loan**) for a specified length of time. For example, if you borrow **$1,000,000** at an interest rate of **7.25%** for **25** years and want to know how much interest you have to pay back within the first month, you can find that out with this formula:

```
=IPMT(7.25%/12; 1; 25*12; 1,000,000)
```

The answer is **–$6041.67**.

	A	B	C	D
202	**IPMT**	**Interest**	**Period**	**Time**
203	IPMT	7.25%	1	300
204				
205		**Loan**	**Future**	**Type**
206		$1,000,000.00	3	0
207				
208	**Result**			
209	-$6,041.67			

Figure 8-6. *Sample result of the IPMT function*

The **period** argument specifies for which accounting period the interest is going to be calculated and the **time** argument is equal to the number of accounting periods. The **future** argument is used to enter the amount of money remaining after the last payment is made. For loans, you usually enter 0 or don't use this argument at all unless you want to use the type argument as well. This is equal to 1 when payments are made at the beginning of each accounting period or equal to 0 when payments are made at the end of each accounting period.

IPMT is similar to **CUMIPMT**, but it calculates interest payable in a single accounting period, whereas **CUMIPMT** calculates the compound interest for one or more accounting periods.

See also the sections on the **PPMT** and **NPER** functions.

Internal Rate of Return (IRR)

Syntax: IRR(Cash Flows; Guess)

The **IRR** function computes the internal rate of return for a given amount of initial investment and a series of cash flows. For example, if you invest **$25,000** in a coffee shop and want to know the internal rate of return for this investment (based on the fact that you received **$30,000**, **$40,000**, **$28,000**, and **$12,000** in return over four years), you should put **–$25,000** (the initial investment) into one cell and all of the income, without the minus sign, in cells below or to the right. If your values are in cells **B212:B216**, you can type the following formula:

```
=IRR(B212:B216)
```

The answer is **120.23%**.

	A	B
211	**IRR**	**Flows**
212	IRR	-$25,000.00
213		$30,000.00
214		$40,000.00
215		$28,000.00
216		$12,000.00
217	**Result**	
218		120.23%

Figure 8-7. Sample result of the IRR function

Not bad for a coffee shop. The **guess** argument is used to specify an estimated value of the internal rate of return for the given series of cash flows.

Nominal Rate of Interest (NOMINAL)

Syntax: NOMINAL(Effective; Periods)

The **NOMINAL** function returns the nominal rate of interest for a given effective rate of interest and the number of payments. So, if you want to check the nominal rate of interest for an effective rate of **10.47%** assuming 12 payment per year, use **=NOMINAL(10.47%; 12)**, which returns **10%**.

	A	B	C	D
220	**NOMINAL**	**Effective**	**Periods**	**Result**
221	NOMINAL	10.47%	12	10.00%

Figure 8-8. Sample result of the NOMINAL function

The opposite of this function is **EFFECTIVE**.

Time to Repay a Loan (NPER)

Syntax: NPER(Interest; Installment; Loan; Future; Type)

If you need an answer to a simple question such as "How many years should it take me to pay the money I borrowed, providing that I pay in equal chunks of money and the interest rate is constant?", the **NPER** function is the right tool to use. Consider the following case: you borrow **$100,000** (**loan**) at an annual rate of interest equal to **7.5%**, and you want to pay back **$10,000** each year. To see how many years it would take you to do this, use this formula:

```
=NPER(7.5%; -10,000; 100,000)
```

which returns **19.17** years!

	A	B	C	D
223	NPER	Interest	Investment	Return
224	NPER	7.50%	-$10,000.00	$100,000.00
225				
226		Future	Type	
227				
228				
229	Result			
230	19.17			

*Figure 8-9. Sample result of the **NPER** function*

The future argument is used to enter the amount of money remaining after the last payment is made. For loans, you usually enter **0**. Don't use this argument at all unless you want to use the **type** argument as well, which is equal to **1** when payments are made at the beginning of each accounting period or equal to **0** when payments are made at the end of each accounting period.

See also the sections on the **IPMT** and **PPMT** functions.

Net Present Value (NPV)

Syntax: NPV(Discount; Value1; Value2; … Value30)

The **NPV** function returns the Net Present Value of an investment. Consider the coffee shop example, discussed previously, in connection with the **IRR** function.

To calculate the value of the investment after four years, you need to put into the **NPV** function the discount rate (such as inflation) and the cash flows for each year. Then, subtract the initial investment from the result of the **NPV**.

Let's assume that income flows are stored in cells **D233:D236** and the initial investment, a negative value, are stored in cell **B233**:

```
=NPV(10%; D233:D236)+B233
```

This returns **$64,563.55**.

	A	B	C	D
232	**NPV**	**Investment**	**Discount**	**Flows**
233	NPV	-$25,000.00	10.00%	$30,000.00
234				$40,000.00
235				$28,000.00
236				$12,000.00
237				
238	**Result**			
239	$64,563.55			

Figure 8-10. *Sample result of the NPV function*

The initial investment ought to be subtracted from the received income. We are adding it because it is a negative value according to OpenOffice.org Calc's convention of marking money paid out as negative with the minus (–) sign and money received as positive (no minus sign).

Now you know how hard your money is working. Another important case is accounting for loss. For example, if your little coffee shop made a loss of **$3,000** in the fifth year, and then a profit of **$20,000** in the sixth year, you'd need to account for that in the following way:

```
=NPV(10%; D233:D236; -3,000; 20,000)+B233
```

And the answer would be **$73,990.27**.

Although it is possible to insert the initial investment into the **NPV** function as a negative value, you really shouldn't do that. This is only valid in cases when we invest at the end of the first accounting period, hardly a typical case, because this assumes that our business venture is running for the first year without any money.

Payment (PMT)

Syntax: PMT(Interest; Time; Loan; Future; Type)

Wondering how much you would have to pay monthly for your mortgage if you agreed to constant monthly repayments? The **PMT** function is the right tool to use. For this use:

```
=PMT(7.5%/12; 25*12; 1,000,000)
```

	A	B	C	D
241	**PMT**	**Interest**	**Time**	**Loan**
242	PMT	7.50%	25	-$1,000,000.00
243				
244		**Future**	**Type**	
245				
246				
247	**Result**			
248	$75,000.00			

Figure 8-11. *Sample result of the PMT function*

In this case you assume that you borrow a cool **$1,000,000** (the **loan**) at a constant interest rate of **7.5%** and you would be paying it back over **25** years. If that's the situation, your monthly rate would be **–$7,389.91**. The minus sign indicates that this is the money paid out of your pocket.

The first argument is the annual **interest** rate that must be divided by **12** if you are making monthly payments, by **4** if payments are made every quarter, or by **2** if payments are made twice a year.

The second argument, **time**, is the total number of payments to be made.

The third argument is the present value of the **loan**.

The last two arguments are the **future** balance after the last payment is made and the **type** of payments (**0** indicates that payments are made at the end of each accounting period, and **1** indicates that payments are made at the beginning of each accounting period).

See also the sections on the **EFFECTIVE**, **IPMT**, **NOMINAL**, and **PPMT** functions.

Capital (PPMT)

Syntax: PPMT(Interest; Period; Time; Loan; Future; Type)

The **PPMT** function returns the amount of original capital that you need to pay back in a given accounting period when you borrow money. For example, if you borrow **$1,000,000** (**loan**) at an interest rate of **7.25%** for **25** years and want to know how much capital you have to pay back within the first month, you can find that out with this formula:

```
=PPMT(7.25%/12; 1; 25*12; 1,000,000)
```

The answer is **–$1,186.40**.

	A	B	C	D
250	**PPMT**	**Interest**	**Period**	**Time**
251	PPMT	7.25%	1	300
252				
253		**Loan**	**Future**	**Type**
254		$1,000,000.00		
255				
256	**Result**			
257	-$1,186.40			

*Figure 8-12. Sample result of the **PPMT** function*

The **interest** argument is the interest rate at which money is borrowed.

The **period** argument is the number of the chosen accounting period, and the **time** argument is the total number of accounting periods.

The present value of a loan is given as the **loan** argument.

The **future** argument is used to enter the amount of money remaining after the last payment is made. For loans, you usually enter **0** or don't use this argument at all unless you want to use the **type** argument as well, which is equal to **1** when payments are made at the beginning of each accounting period or equal to **0** when payments are made at the end of each accounting period.

This function is similar to **CUMPRINC** but calculates the amount of capital that needs to be paid in a single accounting period, and **CUMPRINC** calculates the amount of capital that needs to be paid in one or more accounting periods. See also the section on the **IPMT** function.

This function was known as **IPMT** in StarOffice 5.0 (predecessor to OpenOffice.org). Make sure that the StarOffice Calc 5.0 documents imported into OpenOffice.org Calc contain correct functions.

Present Value (PV)

Syntax: PV(Interest; Time; Installment; Future; Type)

The **PV** function presents the value of an investment. This function returns present value of a series of installments. For example, if you are saving **$100** each month for **25** years and the interest rate is going to be a constant **5%**, your future savings are now worth

`=PV(5%/12; 25*12; -100)`

which is **$17,106.00**.

	A	B	C	D
259	**PV**	**Interest**	**Time**	**Installment**
260	PV	5.00%	25	-$100.00
261				
262		**Deposit**	**Type**	
263		$0.00	0	
264				
265	**Result**			
266	$17,106.00			

Figure 8-13. Sample result of the PV function

The **interest** argument is the annual interest rate (must be divided by **12** if payments are made monthly, or by **4** if payments are made quarterly); the **time** argument is the total number of payment periods.

The **installment** is the amount of money paid at the beginning or the end of each accounting period.

The **future** argument is used to enter the amount of money remaining after the last payment is made. For loans, you usually enter **0** or don't use this argument at all unless you want to use the **type** argument as well, which is equal to **1** when payments are made at the beginning of each accounting period or equal to **0** when payments are made at the end of each accounting period.

See also the section on the **FV** function.

Annual Rate of Interest for Loans (RATE)

Syntax: RATE(Time; Installment; Investment; Future; Type)

Suppose you want to borrow **$1,000,000** and repay it in lump sums of **$100,000** over **25** years. What annual interest rate should the lender set? To find out the answer use

`=RATE(25; -100000; 1,000,000)`

You see that it would be at least **8.78%**.

	A	B	C	D
268	RATE	Time	Installment	Investment
269	RATE		25	-$100,000.00	$1,000,000.00
270				
271		Deposit	Type	
272				
273				
274	Result			
275	8.78%			

*Figure 8-14. Sample result of the **RATE** function*

Do not forget to add a minus sign (–) in front of the payment to indicate the money paid out.
The **future** argument is used to enter the amount of money remaining after the last payment is made. For loans, you usually enter **0** or don't use this argument at all unless you want to use the type argument as well, which is equal to **1** when payments are made at the beginning of each accounting period or equal to **0** when payments are made at the end of each accounting period.

Annual Rate of Interest for Savings (RRI)

Syntax: RRI(Time; Value; Future)

What should the interest rate be if you want your investment of **$100,000** to turn into a nice, round **$1,000,000** over **25** years?

```
=RRI(25; 100,000; 1,000,000)
```

The answer is **9.65%**.

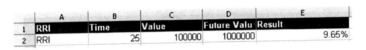

	A	B	C	D	E
1	RRI	Time	Value	Future Valu	Result
2	RRI	25	100000	1000000	9.65%

*Figure 8-15. Sample result of the **RRI** function*

Asset Depreciation

Use these functions to compute depreciation and amortization of assets.

Declining Balance Method (DB)

Syntax: DB(Cost; Salvage; Life; Period; Months)

If you want to use the fixed-declining balance method for calculation of depreciation of assets, this is the function to use. It answers questions such as "What is the depreciation in year x," even if you bought that asset sometime in the middle of the year. For example, when you buy an asset worth **$1,000,000** with a life of **4** years at the beginning of May, you can find its depreciation in year **2** using

=DB(1,000,000; 100; 4; 2; 8)

The answer is **$360,000.00**.

	A	B	C	D
280	**DB**	**Cost**	**Salvage**	**Life**
281	DB	$1,000,000.00	$100.00	4
282				
283		**Period**	**Months**	
284		2	8	
285				
286	**Result**			
287	$360,000.00			

Figure 8-16. *Sample result of the DB function*

The first argument, **cost**, is the price you pay for the asset.

The second, **salvage**, is how much you can get for it (in the preceding example it was **$100**) when you sell it after a certain number of accounting periods (**life**—for yearly depreciation insert the number of years, for monthly—months, and so on).

The **period** argument is the accounting period for which you are trying to find depreciation and the **months** argument is the number of months left in the year you bought the asset (the first year, so even when you buy an asset with a life of **4** years at the beginning of December, you put **4** into the **life** and **1** into the **month** argument).

Double-Declining Balance Method (DDB)

Syntax: DDB(Cost; Salvage; Life; Period; Factor)

This function is similar to **DB**, only it uses the double-declining balance method and lets you set your own depreciation factor, which is set by default to **2**. Using similar data as in the section on the **DB** function, we get these results:

=DDB(1,000,000; 100; 4; 2; 2)

The answer is **$250,000.00**, but if you change the factor to **3**, as in

=DDB(1,000,000; 100; 4; 2; 3)

The result is **$187,500.00**.

	A	B	C	D
289	**DDB**	**Cost**	**Salvage**	**Life**
290	DDB	$1,000,000.00	$100.00	4
291				
292		**Period**	**Months**	
293		2	2	
294				
295	**Result**			
296	$250,000.00			

Figure 8-17. *Sample result of the **DDB** function*

The first argument, **cost**, is the price you pay for the asset.

The second, **salvage**, is how much you can get for it (in the preceding example it was **$100**) when you sell it after a certain number of accounting periods (**life**—for yearly depreciation insert the number of years, for monthly—months, and so on).

The **period** argument is the accounting period for which you are trying to find depreciation.

See also the section on the **VDB** function.

Straight Line Depreciation (SLN)

Syntax: SLN(Cost; Salvage; Life)

The **SLN** function returns the straight line depreciation of an asset for the life of that asset. For example, if you have just bought a brand new Cray supercomputer for the amount of **$1,000,000**, and you know that in three years it should be worth **$1.00**, the value of

=SLN(1,000,000; 1; 3)

results in **$333,333.00**, which you might even be able to write off!

	A	B	C	D	E
298	**SLN**	**Cost**	**Salvage**	**Life**	**Result**
299	SLN	$1,000,000.00	$1.00	$3.00	$333,333.00

Figure 8-18. *Sample result of the **SLN** function*

The first argument, **cost**, is the price you pay for the asset. The second, **salvage**, is how much you can get for it (in the preceding example it was **$1**) when you sell it after a certain number of accounting periods (the **life** argument—for yearly depreciation insert the number of years, for monthly—months, and so on).

Sum-of-Years Method (SYD)

Syntax: SYD(Cost; Salvage; Life; Period)

This function gives asset depreciation using the sum-of-years-digits method. For example:

`=SLD(1,000,000; 100; 4; 2)`

is equal to **$299,970.00**.

	A	B	C	D	E
301	**SYD**	**Cost**	**Salvage**	**Life**	**Period**
302	SYD	$1,000,000.00	$100.00	4	2
303					
304	**Result**				
305	$299,970.00				

Figure 8-19. Sample result of the SYD function

The first argument, **cost**, is the price you pay for the asset.

The second, **salvage**, is how much you can get for it (in the preceding example it was $100) when you sell it after a certain number of accounting periods (the **life** argument—for yearly depreciation insert the number of years, for monthly—months, and so on).

The **period** argument is the accounting period for which you are trying to find depreciation.

Double Declining Curve Method (VDB)

Syntax: VDB(Cost; Salvage; Life; Start_Period; End_Period; Factor; No_Switch)

Asset depreciation for a given period or partial period using the double declining curve is given by this function. This function is similar to **DDB** and lets you set your own depreciation factor (default value is **2**).

Unlike **DDB**, **VDB** enables you to compute depreciation for more than one accounting period. Using similar data as in the section on the **DDB** function, we get these results:

`=VDB(1,000,000; 100; 4; 2; 3; 1; 0)`

which is equal to **$249,966.67**.

	A	B	C	D	E
301	**VDB**	**Cost**	**Salvage**	**Life**	**Start Period**
302	VDB	$1,000,000.00	$100.00	4	2
303					
304		**End Period**	**Factor**	**No Switch**	
305		3	1	0	
306					
307	**Result**				
308	$249,966.67				

Figure 8-20. *Sample result of the VDB function*

The first argument, **cost**, is the price you pay for the asset.

The second, **salvage**, is how much you can get for it (in the preceding example it was **$100**) when you sell it after a certain number of accounting periods (the **life** argument—for yearly depreciation insert the number of years, for monthly—months, and so on).

The **start_period** and **end_period** arguments are used to specify the first and last accounting period used in calculations.

The last two arguments, **factor** and **no_switch**, are used to specify your own depreciation factor and tell OpenOffice.org Calc you want it to automatically switch to the straight line depreciation method when the depreciation is larger than the value for which it was calculated (**no_switch** argument, default value **0**).

See also the section on the **DDB** function.

CHAPTER 9

Formatting Functions

OpenOffice.org Calc can process all sorts of data, including text. The functions presented in this chapter are used to format text that might be formatted in a way that does not suit your needs.

ARABIC

Syntax: ARABIC(text)

The **ARABIC** function converts a text string that contains a Roman numeral into an Arabic number. Roman numerals range from 0 to 3999. It is hard to find them in mainstream use nowadays as the Arabic numbers are much more expressive.

The TV and movie industries use Roman numerals to conceal the age of the material they are showing.

Here is an example of the use of the ARABIC function:

```
=ARABIC("MMXI")
```

returns **2011**.

	A	B	C
1	ARABIC	Text1	Result
2	ARABIC	MMXI	2011

Figure 9-1. *Sample result of the **ARABIC** function*

See also the section on the ROMAN function.

Join Strings of Text (& or CONCATENATE)

Syntax: & or CONCATENATE(text1; text2; … text30)

The **CONCATENATE** function can join up to 30 strings of text. There is no limit for the **&** operator. For example:

```
="Bonnie"&"Clyde"
```

becomes **BonnieClyde**.

If you want to add spaces you need to use a space enclosed in quotation marks (""). For example:

```
="Bonnie"&" "&"Clyde"
```

returns **Bonnie Clyde**.

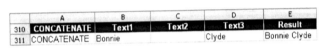

	A	B	C	D	E
310	CONCATENATE	Text1	Text2	Text3	Result
311	CONCATENATE	Bonnie		Clyde	Bonnie Clyde

*Figure 9-2. Sample result of the **CONCATENATE** function*

If these strings were stored in three separate cells, you could also use this notation

```
=A1&A2&A3
```

or

```
=CONCATENATE(B311;C311;D311)
```

assuming that **B311** holds **"Bonnie"**, **C311** holds **" "**, and **D311** holds **"Clyde"**.

CLEAN

Syntax: CLEAN(text)

This removes the non-printable characters from the **text** string. It is useful for cleaning up database files, especially those imported from other operating systems.

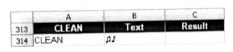

	A	B	C
313	CLEAN	Text	Result
314	CLEAN	♫♪	

*Figure 9-3. Sample result of the **CLEAN** function*

LOWER

Syntax: LOWER(text)

This function turns all given characters into lowercase. For example:

`=LOWER("OpenOffice.org")`

returns **openoffice.org**.

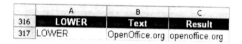

	A	B	C
316	**LOWER**	**Text**	**Result**
317	LOWER	OpenOffice.org	openoffice.org

Figure 9-4. *Sample result of the **LOWER** function*

See also the section on the **UPPER** function.

PROPER

Syntax: PROPER(text)

The **PROPER** function capitalizes the first letter in every word in the given string. For example:

`=PROPER("openoffice.org is cool")`

returns **OpenOffice.org Is Cool**.

	A	B	C
319	**PROPER**	**Text**	
320	PROPER	OpenOffice.org is cool	
321			
322		**Result**	
323		Openoffice.Org Is Cool	

Figure 9-5. *Sample result of the **PROPER** function*

See also the sections on the **LOWER** and **UPPER** functions.

ROMAN

Syntax: ROMAN(number, mode)

The ROMAN function converts an Arabic number into a Roman numeral string. As implemented in OpenOffice.org Calc, Roman numerals can only represent numbers from 0 to 3999; therefore, the number argument cannot be anything else but an integer from that range.

Here is an example of the use of the ROMAN function:

```
=ROMAN(2011)
```

returns **MMXI**.

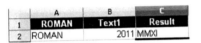

	A	B	C
1	ROMAN	Text1	Result
2	ROMAN	2011	MMXI

Figure 9-6. Sample result of the ROMAN function

The second argument, mode, is an optional numerical value between 0 and 4. It specifies the degree of simplification of the resulting Roman numeral. Think of it as a way to shorten the resulting Roman numerals. Here is an example of how it works:

```
=ROMAN(3999;0)
```

returns **MMMCMXCIX**;

```
=ROMAN(3999;1)
```

returns **MMMLMVLIV**;

```
=ROMAN(3999;2)
```

returns **MMMXMIX**;

```
=ROMAN(3999;3)
```

returns **MMMVMIV**;

```
=ROMAN(3999;4)
```

returns **MMMIM**.

Not all Roman numerals can be simplified, so don't worry if you get the same results with different values of the mode argument.

See also the section on the **ARABIC** function.

TEXT

Syntax: TEXT(number; format)

This function returns a given number as a text string formatted according to the given numeric format. Designing your own format is described in Chapter 4. If you already have a numeric format that you like, simply copy it from the **Format Code** field in the **Cells Format** dialog box into the **Format** field in the **Function Wizard**.

Always remember to put the format string inside double quotes as in this example:

`=TEXT(-1000000; "[$$-409]#,##0.00;[RED]-[$$-409]#,##0.00")`

which returns **–$1,000,000.00**.

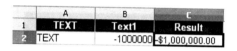

	A	B	C
1	**TEXT**	**Text1**	**Result**
2	TEXT	-1000000	-$1,000,000.00

*Figure 9-7. Sample result of the **TEXT** function*

TRIM

Syntax: TRIM(text)

This function removes extra spaces from strings. For example:

`=TRIM("OpenOffice.org        is        Cool!")`

returns **OpenOffice.org is Cool!**.

	A	B	C
325	**TRIM**	**Text**	
326	TRIM	OpenOffice.org	is cool
327			
328		**Result**	
329		OpenOffice.org is cool	

*Figure 9-8. Sample results of the **TRIM** function*

UPPER

Syntax: UPPER(text)

Upper turns all characters into uppercase. For example:

```
=UPPER("OpenOffice.org")
```

returns **OPENOFFICE.ORG**.

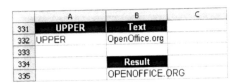

Figure 9-9. Sample results of the UPPER function

See also **LOWER**.

CHAPTER 10

Conversion Functions

This chapter addresses text conversion functions that convert numbers into strings and vice-versa. They are useful for generating strings of text that contain numbers in a specific format. Also included in this chapter are some search functions. Search functions are used many times in conjunction with conversion functions.

Converting Between Numeric Systems (BASE)

Syntax: BASE(Number; Base; Min_Length)

This function converts numbers into text strings that represent the numbers in a different numeric system. It is useful for turning decimal numbers into binary, octal, and hexadecimal numbers. For example:

=BASE(12; 2; 16)

turns number **12** into the string **0000000000001100** (binary number), while

=BASE(12; 8; 16)

turns number **12** into the string **0000000000000014** (octal number), and

=BASE(12; 16; 16)

turns **12** into the string **000000000000000C** (hexadecimal number).

	A	B	C	D
337	**BASE**	**Number**	**Base**	**Min Length**
338	BASE	12	2	16
339				
340	**Result**			
341	0000000000001100			

Figure 10-1. Sample result of the BASE function

As you can see, it is possible to specify the minimum length using the third parameter of the generated string, and the empty spaces are filled with zeroes.

The base argument can be any number from 2 to 36.

Converting Numbers into Currency Strings (DOLLAR)

Syntax: DOLLAR(Value; Decimal_Places)

The **DOLLAR** function converts the given **value** into text in currency format. For example:

```
=DOLLAR(1,000,000; 2)
```

returns **$1,000,000.00**.

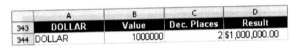

	A	B	C	D
	DOLLAR	**Value**	**Dec. Places**	**Result**
343				
344	DOLLAR	1000000	2	$1,000,000.00

Figure 10-2. Sample result of the DOLLAR function

The second argument indicates the number of places past the **decimal point**. Why is that important? Well, it is good for making headlines such as **A Cool $1,000,000.00 in Sales!**, which you could code as

```
="A cool "&DOLLAR(1,000,000; 2)&" in Sales!"
```

Adding Thousand Separators (FIXED)

Syntax: FIXED(Number; Decimal_Places; No_Commas)

The **FIXED** function converts the given number into comma-separated text format. For example:

```
=FIXED(1000000; 2)
```

returns **1,000,000.00** unless you put **1** as the third argument to switch commas off.

	A	B	C	D
	FIXED	**Value**	**Dec. Places**	**Result**
346				
347	FIXED	1000000	2	1,000,000.00

Figure 10-3. Sample result of the FIXED function

The second argument, **decimal_places**, is used to specify the number of decimal places. For an idea on how to use this function, see **DOLLAR**.

Searching for Strings (FIND – Case-Sensitive)

Syntax: FIND(Find_Text; Source_Text; Start_From)

This function finds the starting position of the specified text string (**find_text**) within another text string (**source_text**). For example:

`=FIND("Office"; "OpenOffice.org")`

returns **5**, the starting position of the **Office** string within the **OpenOffice.org** string.

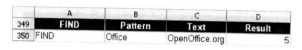

	A	B	C	D
	FIND	Pattern	Text	Result
349				
350	FIND	Office	OpenOffice.org	5

Figure 10-4. Sample result of the FIND function

The third, optional argument start_from is used to specify the starting position within **source_text** from which **FIND** begins looking for the **find_text** string.

Replacing Strings (REPLACE)

Syntax: REPLACE(Old_Text; Start_Number; Number_of_Chars; New_Text)

This function replaces part of a string **old_text** with a new string **new_text**, as in

`=REPLACE("OpenOffice.org"; 5; 10; "Calc")`

which returns **OpenCalc**.

	A	B	C	D
352	REPLACE	Old Text	Start	Number
353	REPLACE	OpenOffice.org	5	10
354				
355		Replacement		Result
356		Calc		OpenCalc

Figure 10-5. Sample result of the REPLACE function

The two numeric arguments (**start_number** and **number_of_chars**) are the position where the replacement ought to begin and the number of characters that are to be replaced.

Searching for Strings (SEARCH – Case-Insensitive)

Syntax: SEARCH(Find_Text; Source_Text; Start_Number)

The **SEARCH** function finds the specified text string, **find_text**, within another text string, **source_text**, but unlike **FIND**, this function is not case-sensitive. For example:

```
=FIND("office"; "OpenOffice.org")
```

returns error **#VALUE!**, meaning the search term was not found, but

```
=SEARCH("office"; "OpenOffice.org")
```

returns **5**, the starting position of the **Office** string within the **OpenOffice.org** string.

	A	B	C	D
358	**SEARCH**	**Pattern**	**Text**	**Result**
359	SEARCH	office	OpenOffice.org	5

Figure 10-6. Sample result of the SEARCH function

The **start_number** argument enables you to change the position from which the search begins (default value is **1**).

Selectively Replacing Strings (SUBSTITUTE)

Syntax: SUBSTITUTE(Source_Text; Substring; New_Text; Occurrence)

The **SUBSTITUTE** function is similar to **REPLACE**, only here you can choose which occurrence of **substring** is to be replaced. For example:

```
=SUBSTITUTE("OpenOffice.org Is Cool! OpenOffice.org Calc Is Cool!"; "Is"; "Is Way"; 2)
```

returns **OpenOffice.org Is Cool! OpenOffice.org Calc Is Way Cool!**

	A	B	C	D	E
361	**SUBSTITUTE**	**Source**			
362	SUBSTITUTE	OpenOffice.org Is Cool! OpenOffice.org Calc Is Cool!			
363					
364		**Substring**			
365		Is			
366					
367		**Replacement**			
368		Is Way			
369					
370		**Occurrence**			
371		2			
372					
373		**Result**			
374		OpenOffice.org Is Cool! OpenOffice.org Calc Is Way Cool!			

*Figure 10-7. Sample result of the **SUBSTITUTE** function*

The **source_text** argument is the text string where you need to find a substring to be replaced with **new_text**. The **occurrence** argument is used to specify which **substring** ought to be replaced.

Conditional Functions

Conditional functions are used to add some built-in "artificial intelligence" to your worksheets. They compare text strings and their results (**true** or **false**) can be used to change the appearance of the worksheet or the way calculations are done.

Comparing Strings (EXACT)

Syntax: EXACT(t1; t2)

EXACT compares two strings and returns **1** if they are exactly the same or **0** if they are not. For example:

```
=EXACT("OpenOffice.org"; "OpenOffice.org")
```

returns **1**, while

```
=EXACT("OpenOffice.org"; "openoffice.org")
```

returns **0**.

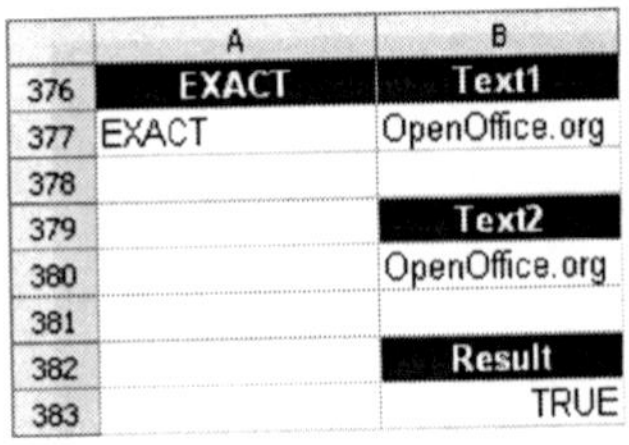

	A	B
376	**EXACT**	**Text1**
377	EXACT	OpenOffice.org
378		
379		**Text2**
380		OpenOffice.org
381		
382		**Result**
383		TRUE

Figure 10-8. *Sample result of the* ***EXACT*** *function*

CHAPTER 11

Utility Functions

Utility functions discussed in this chapter are used to perform various formatting chores and return useful information about text strings. They can help you in analysis of textual data, making OpenOffice.org Calc an even more useful tool.

ASCII Character (CHAR)

Syntax: CHAR(Number)

The **CHAR** function returns an ASCII character whose **number** is **0** to **255**. For example:

`=CHAR(64)`

returns the character **@**.

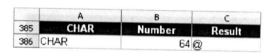

	A	B	C
385	**CHAR**	**Number**	**Result**
386	CHAR	64	@

*Figure 11-1. Sample result of the **CHAR** function*

The characters displayed on screen may differ depending on the system's language and display font settings.

ASCII Code (CODE)

Syntax: CODE(Text)

The **CODE** function returns the code of the first character in the given string. For example:

`=CODE("OpenOffice.org")`

returns **32**.

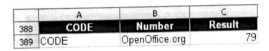

*Figure 11-2. Sample result of the **CODE** function*

Left-Side Substring (LEFT)

Syntax: LEFT(Text; n)

The **LEFT** function returns the first character from the string text, or a specified number of **n** characters starting from the left. For example:

`=LEFT("OpenOffice.org")`

returns **O**, and

`=LEFT("OpenOffice.org"; 4)`

returns **Open**.

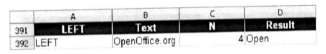

*Figure 11-3. Sample result of the **LEFT** function*

See also **MID** and **RIGHT**.

Length of a String (LEN)

Syntax: LEN(Text)

The **LEN** function returns the length of the given string. For example:

`=LEN("OpenOffice.org")`

returns **14**.

	A	B	C
394	LEN	Text	Result
395	LEN	OpenOffice.org	14

Figure 11-4. Sample result of the LEN function

Middle (MID)

Syntax: MID(Text; Start; n)

The **MID** function returns a substring of the **text** string, starting from the **start** position and containing a given number of characters (**n**). For example:

=MID("OpenOffice.org"; 2; 6)

returns **penOff**.

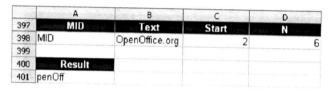

	A	B	C	D
397	MID	Text	Start	N
398	MID	OpenOffice.org	2	6
399				
400	Result			
401	penOff			

Figure 11-5. Sample results of the MID function

See also **LEFT** and **RIGHT**.

Repeat String (REPT)

Syntax: REPT(Text; Repetitions)

The **REPT** function creates a string that consists of a given string (**text**) repeated (**n**) number of times. For example:

=REPT("Open"; 4)

returns **OpenOpenOpenOpen**.

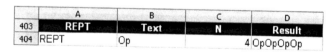

	A	B	C	D
403	REPT	Text	N	Result
404	REPT	Op	4	OpOpOpOp

Figure 11-6. Sample results of the REPT function

Right-Side Substring (RIGHT)

Syntax: RIGHT(Text; n)

The **RIGHT** function returns the last **n** characters from the end of the string text, or a specified number of characters (**n**) starting from the right. For example:

`=RIGHT("OpenOffice.org", 4)`

returns **.org** and

`=RIGHT("OpenOffice.org"; 6)`

returns **ce.org**.

	A	B	C	D
406	**RIGHT**	**Text**	**N**	**Result**
407	RIGHT	OpenOffice.org	4	.org

Figure 11-7. Sample results of the RIGHT function

See also **LEFT** and **MID**.

Obfuscate (ROT13)

Syntax: ROT13(Text)

The **ROT13** function encrypts text using a simple algorithm called Caesar's Code, where each letter is replaced by one of the **13** characters in the Latin alphabet.
Rotating the encoded text by **13** again returns the original string. For example:

`=ROT13("OpenOffice.org")`

returns **BcraBssvpr.bet**, while

`=ROT13(ROT13("OpenOffice.org"))`

returns **OpenOffice.org**.

	A	B	C
409	**ROT13**	**Text**	**Result**
410	ROT13	OpenOffice.org	BcraBssvpr.bet

Figure 11-8. Sample results of the ROT13 function

It is not a very strong form of protecting data, but it is enough to keep it from being accidentally revealed to someone who might be "just looking."

Return Text Values Only (T)

Syntax: T(Value)

The **T** function is a bit strange. It returns the text string given to it as its argument. For example:

=T("OpenOffice.org")

returns **OpenOffice.org**, but

=T(10)

returns **""** because **10** is not a text string.

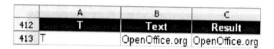

	A	B	C
412	T	Text	Result
413	T	OpenOffice.org	OpenOffice.org

Figure 11-9. Sample results of the T function

This function is obsolete and it is here only because of compatibility requirements with the previous OpenOffice spreadsheet software.

CHAPTER 12

Time & Date Functions

We all know what dates are and what we mean when we say "I need it done in three days," but such natural expressions are not so easy for computers. Unfortunately, computations that involve time and dates are essential in business and cannot be ignored. Without them it would be very difficult to judge the potential profitability of a planned business venture, the real cost of a loan, or the future value of an investment.

A lot of financial functions greatly benefit from the use of date functions, because they make it possible to automate a lot of time-based calculations. Automating things is always a good idea, because it saves you time and money.

There are two kinds of OpenOffice.org Calc time-related functions: **date functions** (for bigger chunks of time: days, weeks, months, or years) and **time functions** (for shorter periods of time: hours, minutes, or seconds). That distinction exists for your own comfort only, because all date and time calculations in OpenOffice.org Calc are based on the same fractional number (a.k.a. "timestamp") that represents the number of seconds that have elapsed since a subjectively chosen moment in time called an Epoch, which is a fancy way of saying the time counter value was equal to **00:00:00.00** (i.e., zero).

You can set the Epoch yourself (choose **Tools ➤ Options** and select the **Calculate** item in the **OpenOffice.org Calc** branch to display a panel where you can choose one of the three available Epochs) (see the **Date** section in Figure 12-1).

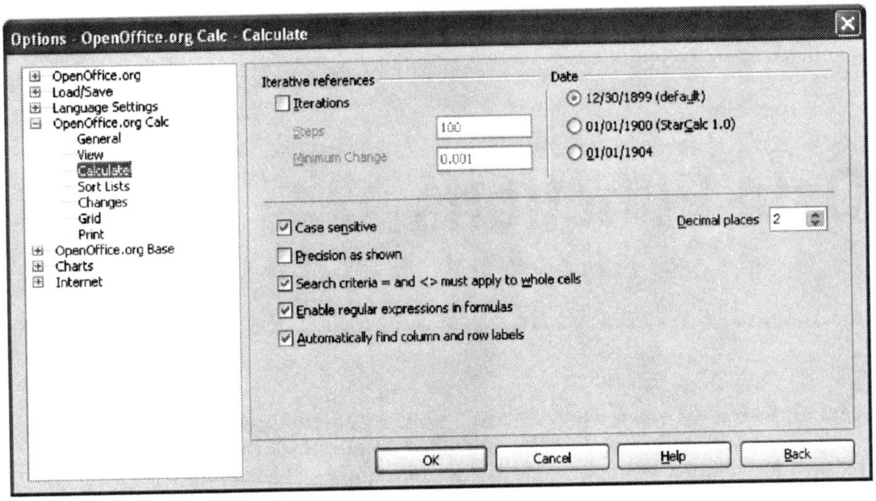

Figure 12-1. Set the Epoch in the Date section.

Unless you have old documents created well before the year **2000**, you should always use the default Epoch of **12/30/1899**.

Whichever Epoch you choose, the count starts at midnight. For the standard Epoch, OpenOffice.org Calc can recognize years between **1583** and **9956**, or, if you enter them as two-digit years, from 19**XX** to 20**XX**–1. If you decide to use the shorter notation, i.e., **12/15/20** instead of **12/15/2020**, you will have to tell OpenOffice.org Calc how it should convert two-digit years into four-digit years.

You do this in the **Options** dialog box in the **General** branch (choose **Tools ➤ Options**) as shown in Figure 12-2.

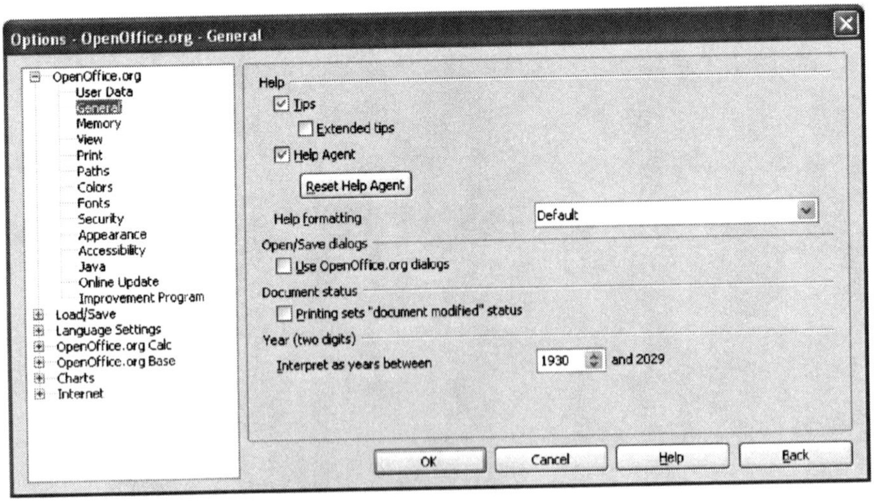

Figure 12-2. Set two-digit years in the Year section.

When you change Epochs or the two-year conversion settings always do it before opening or creating a worksheet to make sure that the dates are interpreted in a consistent manner.

The date functions can be divided into the following groups:

- Functions that return a timestamp.

- Functions that extract date components.

- Functions that calculate the difference between dates.

Functions that Return a Timestamp

Date and time information is stored on modern computer systems as a fractional number called a timestamp. It is commonly set to the number of seconds that have elapsed from midnight January 1, 1970.

All date and time calculations are done much faster on timestamps than the date or time written the way we are used to, because a single number is easier to process. For example, to find out the difference between two dates, it is sufficient to subtract two timestamps instead of comparing six numbers (two years, two months, and two days).

To make it easy to work with timestamps, we need a helper function like **DATE**. It is less often used today than a few years ago thanks to the maturity of the OpenOffice.org Calc code.

Timestamp (DATE)

Syntax: DATE(Year; Month; Day)

The **DATE** function returns the timestamp for the given year, month, and day. To test it, place the following formula into any empty cell on the current worksheet:

`=DATE(2010; 1; 1)`

The result should be **40179**.

	A	B	C	D
415	**DATE**	**Year**	**Month**	**Day**
416	DATE	2010	1	1
417				
418	**Result**			
419	40179			

Figure 12-3. *Sample result of the DATE function*

If you see a date like **01/01/10**, which is not what you wanted in this case, change the numeric formatting of that cell to **Text**. In order to do that, choose **Format ➤ Cells** and click on the **Numbers** tab to change the numeric format for that cell to **Text / @**. The value of the timestamp might be different if you use a non-default Epoch.

One useful trick that you might want to remember is using the **DATE** function to automatically calculate the timestamp of a day in a year's time. For example:

```
=DATE((YEAR(TODAY())+1); MONTH(TODAY()); DAY(TODAY()))
```

The formula shown above is useful if you are trying to do financial and other calculations based on time.

Today's Timestamp (TODAY)

Syntax: TODAY()

This useful function returns the timestamp to the current day. For example, on January 3, 2010:

```
=TODAY()
```

returns **40181**.

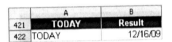

*Figure 12-4. Sample result of the **TODAY** function*

You can use this function in a worksheet that calculates mortgage payment schedules for your clients. Instead of typing in a new date into a formula calculating mortgage payments, put **TODAY** into the start date values and it will save you a lot of time. You can be even more inventive and add or subtract a certain number of days to construct even more flexible formulas:

```
=TODAY()+30
```

This formula will regenerate the timestamp for a date 30 days from today. If you replace the hard number with a cell reference (e.g., **A2**), you will make the formula even more flexible, because you will not have to rewrite it every time you change the number of days you want to add or subtract:

```
=TODAY()+A2
```

See also the descriptions of financial functions such as **FV** and **PV** in Chapter 8 for an example on how to use **TODAY**.

Extracting Date Components

Some date and time operations are surprisingly inconvenient. For example, if you have ever had to find out the week number for a date, you know how time-consuming such a simple task can be. The following functions help with such mundane tasks.

Extracting Days from a Date (DAY)

Syntax: DAY(t)

The **DAY** function is used to convert a date given in any recognizable format into a day of the month. For example:

```
=DAY(40179)
```

returns **1** (January 1, 2010).

	A	B	C
424	**DAY**	**Timestamp**	**Result**
425	DAY	40179	1

*Figure 12-5. Sample result of the **DAY** function*

You can give **DAY** the date in a more natural format:

```
=DAY("3/17/2010")
```

returns **17** (March 17, 2010).

See the description of the **DATE** function for another example of using the **DAY** function in practice.

Extracting Weekdays from a Date (WEEKDAY)

Syntax: WEEKDAY(t; Day)

The **WEEKDAY** function is used to convert a date given in any recognizable format into a day of the week. Days are numbered from **0** (Sunday) to **6** (Saturday). For example:

```
=WEEKDAY("1/1/2010")
```

returns **6**.

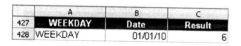

	A	B	C
427	**WEEKDAY**	**Date**	**Result**
428	WEEKDAY	01/01/10	6

*Figure 12-6. Sample result of the **WEEKDAY** function*

This result is produced by **WEEKDAY** assuming that weeks start on Sunday (day **0**).

You can modify those results with the **day** argument. Its values can be as follows:

- 1: week starts on Sunday (day **0**).

- 2: weeks start on Monday (day **1**).

- 3: weeks start on Monday (day **0**).

Compare the following formulas and their results for the same date:

`=WEEKDAY("1/1/2010"; 1)`

returns **6**;

`=WEEKDAY("1/1/2010"; 2)`

returns **5**; and

`=WEEKDAY("1/1/2010"; 3)`

returns **4**.

Extract Week Number from a Date (WEEKNUM)

Syntax: WEEKNUM(t; Day)

The **WEEKNUM** function is used to convert a date given in any recognizable format into the appropriate week number. You need to specify the first day of the week using an integer number (Sunday is **1**, Monday is **2**). For example:

`=WEEKNUM("2/7/2010"; 2)`

returns **5**, and

`=WEEKNUM("2/7/2010"; 1)`

returns **6**.

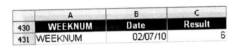

	A	B	C
430	WEEKNUM	Date	Result
431	WEEKNUM	02/07/10	6

*Figure 12-7. Sample result of the **WEEKNUM** function*

Extract Month from a Date (MONTH)

Syntax: MONTH(t)

The **MONTH** function is used to convert a date given in any recognizable format into the month number. For example:

```
=MONTH(DATE(2010; 6; 27))
```

returns **6**.

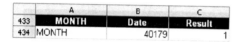

Figure 12-8. *Sample result of the* **MONTH** *function*

You can give **MONTH** the date in a more natural format:

```
=MONTH("3/17/2010")
```

returns **3** (March 17, 2010).

See the description of the **DATE** function for another example of using the **MONTH** function in practice.

Extract Year from a Date (YEAR)

Syntax: YEAR(t)

The **YEAR** function is used to convert a date given in any recognizable format into a year number. For example:

```
=YEAR(DATE(2010; 11; 1))
```

returns **2010**.

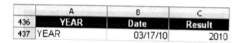

Figure 12-9. *Sample result of the* **YEAR** *function*

You can give **YEAR** the date in a more natural format:

=YEAR("3/17/2010")

returns **2010** (March 17, 2010).
See the description of the **DATE** function, Number of Days in a Month (DAYSINMONTH).

Syntax: DAYSINMONTH(t)

The **DAYSINMONTH** function returns the number of days in the given date. For example:

=DAYSINMONTH(DATE(2012; 2; 16))

returns **29** (February 2012 has 29 days because the year 2012 is a leap year).

	A	B	C
439	**DAYSINMONTH**	**Date**	**Result**
440	DAYSINMONTH	02/16/12	29

*Figure 12-10. Sample result of the **DAYSINMONTH** function*

You can give **DAYSINMONTH** the date in a more natural format:

=DAYSINMONTH("2/16/2012")

returns **29** again.

Number of Days in a Year (DAYSINYEAR)

Syntax: DAYSINYEAR(t)

The **DAYSINYEAR** function returns the number of days in the given date. For example:

=DAYSINYEAR(DATE(2012; 2; 16))

returns **366** (because the year **2012** is a leap year).

	A	B	C
442	**DAYSINYEAR**	**Date**	**Result**
443	DAYSINYEAR	02/16/12	366

*Figure 12-11. Sample result of the **DAYSINYEAR** function*

You can give **DAYSINYEAR** the date in a more natural format:

`=DAYSINYEAR("2/16/2012")`

returns **366** again.

Number of Weeks in a Year (WEEKSINYEAR)

Syntax: WEEKSINYEAR(t)

The **WEEKSINYEAR** function returns the number of weeks in the given date. For example:

`=WEEKSINYEAR(DATE(2012; 2; 16))`

returns **52**.

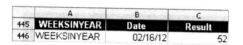

	A	B	C
445	**WEEKSINYEAR**	**Date**	**Result**
446	WEEKSINYEAR	02/16/12	52

*Figure 12-12. Sample result of the **WEEKSINYEAR** function*

You can give **WEEKSINYEAR** the date in a more natural format:

`=WEEKSINYEAR("2/16/2012")`

returns **52** again.

Functions that Calculate the Difference Between Two Dates

Another handy set of functions are those that calculate the difference between two dates, which is often used to compute interest or discount in financial calculations.

Difference Between Two Dates in Real Units (DAYS)

Syntax: DAYS(t1; t2)

The **DAYS** function calculates the number of days between two dates. For example:

`=DAYS("12/15/2010"; NOW())`

returns **–383.93**, on Nov. 26, 2009 at 1:35 a.m.

You can give **DAYS** the date in a more natural format:

`=DAYS(DATE(2010; 12; 15); NOW())`

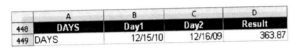

	A	B	C	D
448	**DAYS**	**Day1**	**Day2**	**Result**
449	DAYS	12/15/10	12/16/09	363.87

Figure 12-13. Sample result of the DAYS function

The minus sign appears in the result because OpenOffice.org Calc always subtracts **t2** from **t1 (t1 – t2)**.

Remember that you can remove the minus sign with the **ABS** function, but you need to watch out for errors that such shortcuts may introduce to your calculations:

`=ABS(DAYS("12/15/2010"; NOW()))`

The **DAYS** function is useful for calculating short-term interest when money is borrowed for days rather than months or years.

It is important to remember that these calculations are based on a calendar year with **365** or **366** days (leap years).

See also the description of the **DAYS360** function.

Difference Between Two Dates in Banker's Units (DAYS360)

Syntax: DAYS360(t1; t2; Year_Type)

The **DAYS360** function calculates the number of days between two dates given as timestamps, in banker's years. For example:

`=DAYS360(DATE(2010; 1; 15); DATE(2010; 6; 1); 0)`

returns **136**.

You can give **DAYS360** the date in a more natural format:

`=DAYS360("1/15/2010"; "6/1/2010"; 0)`

	A	B	C	D
451	**DAYS360**	**Day1**	**Day2**	**Year Type**
452	DAYS360	01/15/10	06/01/10	0
453				
454	**Result**			
455	136			

Figure 12-14. Sample result of the DAYS360 function

The banker's year has 12 months of 30 days each giving a total of 360 days in a year. It was, and sometimes still is, used before banks started using computers. It simplifies calculations when they are done by hand, but it is not fair to the banks or the borrowers.

The last number in the **DAYS360** function ought to be **0** or **1**, depending on which, European (**1**) or American (**0**), kind of 360-day year you want to use.

If you need to use the **DAYS360** function, always make sure that you choose the right system. See also the description of the **DAYS** function.

Number of Months Between Two Dates (MONTHS)

Syntax: MONTHS(t1; t2)

The **MONTHS** function calculates the number of months between two dates, either in monthly intervals (**0**) or in calendar months (**1**). For example:

```
=MONTHS(DATE(2010; 1; 15); DATE(2010; 2; 1); 0)
```

returns **0**, because the difference between these two dates is less than the length of one full month, and

```
=MONTHS(DATE(2010; 1; 15); DATE(2010; 2; 1); 1)
```

returns **1**, because in calendar terms there is a difference of one month (in February, we think of January 15 as last month's date).

	A	B	C	D
457	MONTHS	Day1	Day2	Month Type
458	MONTHS	01/15/10	02/01/10	0
459				
460	Result			
461	0			

*Figure 12-15. Sample result of the **MONTHS** function*

You can give **MONTHS** the date in a more natural format:

```
=MONTHS("1/15/2010"; "2/1/2010"; 0)
```

Number of Weeks Between Two Dates (WEEKS)

Syntax: WEEKS(t1; t2; Week_Type)

The **WEEKS** function calculates the number of weeks between two dates, either in weekly intervals (**0**) or in calendar weeks (**1**). For example:

```
=WEEKS(DATE(2010; 1; 15); DATE(2010; 2; 1); 0)
```

returns **2**, because the difference between these two dates is less than the length of three full weeks (**21** days), and

```
=WEEKS(DATE(2010; 1; 15); DATE(2010; 2; 1); 1)
```

returns **3**, because in calendar terms in February we think of January 15 as being three weeks ago.

	A	B	C	D
463	**WEEKS**	**Day1**	**Day2**	**Week Type**
464	WEEKS	01/15/10	02/01/10	0
465				
466	**Result**			
467	2			

Figure 12-16. Sample result of the WEEKS function

You can give **WEEKS** the date in a more natural format:

```
=WEEKS("1/15/2010"; "2/1/2010"; 0)
```

Number of Months Between Two Dates (YEARS)

Syntax: YEARS(t1; t2; Year_Type)

The **YEARS** function calculates the number of years between two dates, either in yearly intervals (**0**) or calendar years (**1**). For example:

```
=YEARS(DATE(2009; 12; 31); DATE(2010; 1; 1); 0)
```

returns **0**, because the difference between these two dates is less than the length of a full year, and

```
=YEARS(DATE(2009; 12; 31); DATE(2010; 1; 1); 1)
```

returns **1**, because in calendar terms there is a difference of one year between those two dates.

	A	B	C	D
469	**YEARS**	**Day1**	**Day2**	**Year Type**
470	YEARS	12/31/09	01/01/10	0
471				
472	**Result**			
473	0			

Figure 12-17. Sample results of the YEARS function

You can give **YEARS** the date in a more natural format:

```
=YEARS("12/31/2010"; "1/1/2010"; 0)
```

All of these functions may or may not be influenced by the Epoch setting. They are affected if you mix dates from different worksheets with different Epochs and enter or reference timestamps directly into a function or formula, such as **WEEKDAY(36526; 1)**. To prevent this from happening, use the **DAY** function to provide correct timestamps.

CHAPTER 13

Conditional Functions

All of the functions that were discussed in the previous chapters of this book work in a fairly simple way. You give them some input and they process it and return a single value. Useful, but not what we would call "smart."

If you want your worksheets to be smart, you need to use conditional functions that can make decisions based on a set of pre-defined conditions.

Tax returns are one good example of the need for a worksheet to be smart. Let's assume that we want to use just two cells in a sheet, one to enter the amount of money to be taxed and the other to display the amount of tax due. Use the following imaginary income tax rates:

- A tax free allowance of $5,000.

- 20% tax on any amount above $5,000.

- 30% tax on any amount above $20,000.

What you need to compute the correct amount of tax is a formula that can make decisions based on the amount of taxable income. If you were to explain them to somebody, you would say:

- If the amount of taxable income is $5,000 or less, there is no tax to pay.

- If the amount of taxable income is greater than $5,000 but not greater than $20,000, subtract $5,000 from the amount of taxable income. The income tax payable on the remaining amount of taxable income is 20%.

- If the amount of taxable income is greater than $20,000, subtract $20,000 from the amount of taxable income. The income tax payable on the remaining amount of taxable income is 30% + $3,000.

As you can see, even a simple set of rules like these can take quite a few sentences to explain. That can be problematic for computers, because they like short, precise instructions.

Fortunately, there is a way to describe various conditions in a simple, terse format using the **IF** function and a set of relational operators discussed in the following sections of this chapter.

Making Decisions (IF)

Syntax: IF(Test; True; False)

The most important of all conditional functions used in OpenOffice.org Calc is **IF**. It takes three arguments:

- **Test**: the condition you want to test for.

- **True**: what **IF** returns when **test** returns **TRUE**.

- **False**: what **IF** returns when **test** returns **FALSE**.

In the case of the tax rates mentioned on the previous page, you need to build a nested formula that uses more than one **IF** function. Let's do it one step at a time.

The first condition is for the **$5,000** exemption. Put the taxable income into cell **A2** and the tax-free allowance into cell **B2**. The formula will look like the following one and in Figure 13-1. You can put it anywhere, but for the purpose of this exercise it will be cell **A5**:

```
=IF(A2 > B2; "Add another IF here"; 0)
```

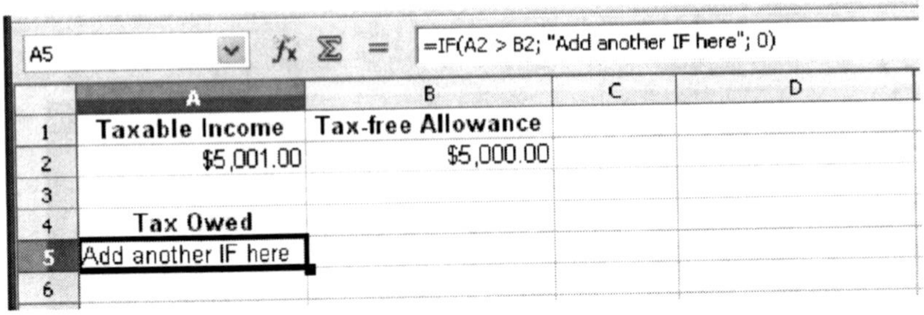

Figure 13-1. *Testing for the tax-free allowance*

The text that appears in cell **A5** after you enter a number greater than the tax-free allowance stored in cell **B2** needs to be replaced with another test implemented as a nested **IF** function. In this case, you drop the = sign from the front of the nested function. You will now add the first taxable income tier and rate and implement it in the following way:

```
=IF(A2 > B2;
        IF(A2 <= C2; (A2-B2)*D2; "Second tier");
        0)
```

A5		✓	*fx* Σ =	=IF(A2 > B2; IF(A2<=C2;(A2-B2)*D2;"Second tier"); 0)

	A	B	C	D
1	Taxable Income	Tax-free Allowance	First Tier	First Tier Tax Rate
2	$5,001.00	$5,000.00	$20,000.00	20.00%
3				
4	Tax Owed			
5	$0.20			
6				

Figure 13-2. Testing for the first tax tier

Because you cannot use multiline formulas in OpenOffice.org Calc, you need to enter the new formula into cell **A5** in the following way:

```
=IF(A2 > B2; IF(A2 <= C2; (A2-B2)*D2; "Second tier"); 0)
```

As you can see, there is a placeholder (second tier) for the values of taxable income greater than the value stored in cell **C2** (first tier) and the placeholder will be replaced with another formula for taxable income greater than $20,000:

```
=IF(A2 > B2;
        IF(A2 <= C2;
                (A2-B2)*D2;
                (C2-B2)*D2+(A2-C2)*F2);
        0)
```

That formula has to be typed as a single line of text into cell **A5**:

```
=IF(A2 > B2; IF(A2 <= C2; (A2-B2)*D2; (C2-B2)*D2+(A2-C2)*F2); 0)
```

A5		✓	*fx* Σ =	=IF(A2 > B2; IF(A2<=C2;(A2-B2)*D2;(C2-B2)*D2+(A2-C2)*F2); 0)		

	A	B	C	D	E	F
1	Taxable Income	Tax-free Allowance	First Tier	First Tier Tax Rate	Second Tier	Second Tier Tax Rate
2	$20,001.00	$5,000.00	$20,000.00	20.00%		30.00%
3						
4	Tax Owed					
5	$3,000.30					
6						

Figure 13-3. Testing for the second tax tier

As you can see in Figure 13-3, there is another cell (**E2**) not in use. It is there in case you need to add another tax tier.

Please note that the example given in this section is not based on any particular tax code. Check your local tax code for guidance on tax rates, tax tiers, and ways of computing taxes.

Relational Operators

Relational operators are used inside the **IF** function to compare two values. They represent six basic tests that can be employed to construct a conditional formula.

The following examples show formulas that display the first text string if a condition is met or the second string if the condition is not met.

- **Equal: =**—**A1** and **A2** are equal:

  `=IF(A1=A2; "A1 is equal to A2"; "A1 and A2 not equal")`

- **Less than: <**—**A1** is less than **A2**:

  `=IF(A1<A2; "A1 is less than A2"; "A1 is not less than A2")`

- **Greater than: >**—**A1** is greater than **A2**:

  `=IF(A1>A2; "A1 is greater than A2"; "A1 is not greater than A2")`

- **Less than or equal to: <=**—**A1** is less than or equal to **A2**:

  `=IF(A1<=A2; "A1 is less than or equal to A2"; "A1 is not less than or equal to A2")`

- **Greater than or equal to: >=**—**A1** is greater than or equal to **A2**:

  `=IF(A1>=A2; "A1 is greater than or equal to A2"; "A1 is not greater than or equal to A2")`

- **Different from: <>**—**A1** is not equal to **A2**:

  `=IF(A1<>A2; "A1 is different than A2"; "A1 is not different than A2")`

Logical Functions

Logical functions can be used to build long and complex conditional formulas where more than one test is required.

AND

Syntax: AND(Cond_1; Cond_2; … Cond_30)

This function is used to compare results of up to 30 (thirty) conditions. The value of **AND** is **TRUE** if all of the conditions tested are **TRUE** as well. For example, the following formula is **TRUE** only if **A1** is equal to **A2** and **A3**, otherwise, it is **FALSE**:

`=AND(A1=A2; A2=A3)`

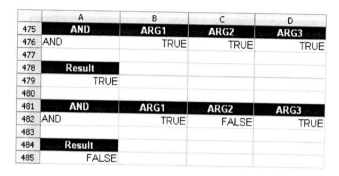

	A	B	C	D
475	**AND**	**ARG1**	**ARG2**	**ARG3**
476	AND	TRUE	TRUE	TRUE
477				
478	**Result**			
479	TRUE			
480				
481	**AND**	**ARG1**	**ARG2**	**ARG3**
482	AND	TRUE	FALSE	TRUE
483				
484	**Result**			
485	FALSE			

*Figure 13-4. Sample results of the **AND** function*

FALSE

Syntax: FALSE()

This function returns the logical value of **FALSE**.
See also the section on the **TRUE** function.

NOT

Syntax: NOT(Logic_Value)

NOT negates logical values, so **FALSE** becomes **TRUE** and **TRUE** becomes **FALSE**, as in these examples:

=NOT(1<>1)

returns **TRUE**, and

=NOT(1=1)

returns **FALSE**.

	A	B	C
487	**NOT**	**Value**	**Result**
488	NOT	TRUE	FALSE
489	NOT	FALSE	TRUE

*Figure 13-5. Sample results of the **NOT** function*

OR

Syntax: OR(Cond_1; Cond_2; ... Cond_30)

The **OR** function is used to compare results of up to 30 (thirty) conditions. The value of **OR** is **TRUE** if at least one of the conditions tested is **TRUE**. For example, the following formula

```
=OR(A1=A2; A2=A3)
```

is **TRUE** if **A1** is equal to **A2**, if **A2** is equal to **A3**, or if **A1** is equal to **A2** and **A3**. If **A1** is not equal to **A2**, and **A2** is not equal to **A3**, the formula is **FALSE**.

	A	B	C	D
491	**OR**	**ARG1**	**ARG2**	**ARG3**
492	OR	TRUE	TRUE	TRUE
493				
494	**Result**			
495	TRUE			
496				
497	**OR**	**ARG1**	**ARG2**	**ARG3**
498	OR	TRUE	FALSE	TRUE
499				
500	**Result**			
501	TRUE			

Figure 13-6. Sample results of the OR function

TRUE

Syntax: TRUE()

The **TRUE** function returns logical value of **TRUE**.
　　　See also the section on the **FALSE** function.

Index

CPSIA information can be obtained at www.ICGtesting.com
Printed in the USA
LVOW132354031011

248961LV00009B/16/P